Reco
Healing and Peace *in* South Sudan

Reflections on the Way Forward

Barani Eduardo
Hiiboro Kussala

Paulines

PAULINES PUBLICATIONS AFRICA

RECONCILIATION, HEALING AND PEACE IN SOUTH SUDAN
© St Paul Communications/Daughters of St Paul
ISBN 9966-08-897-0
Year of publication 2015

PAULINES PUBLICATIONS AFRICA
Daughters of St Paul
P.O. Box 49026
00100 Nairobi GPO (Kenya)
E-mail: publications@paulinesafrica.org
Website: www.paulinesafrica.org

Cover Design by Elizabeth Wamũcii Kagwe
Layout and Typesetting by Antony M. Wamwaki

Printed by Don Bosco Printing Press, P.O. Box 158, Makuyu Kenya)
Email: press@ofmconvkenya.org

Contents

CHAPTER THREE
Negotiation in a Time of Crisis

CHAPTER FOUR
Restorative Justice: A New Vocabulary

CHAPTER FIVE
Reconciliation: A Gift from God for Humanity

Preface

This book by Bishop Hiiboro Eduardo Dr Kussala, which sketches the beginnings of the South Sudanese nation's emergence as a country, is a welcome contribution to the indispensable struggle for reconciliation and peace in the country. It is fully in keeping with the pastoral activities of the Local Church of South Sudan. The responsibility of safeguarding life and hailing the promotion of Justice and Peace has been at the heart of the teachings of the Sudanese bishops.

This book, *"Reconciliation, Healing and Peace in South Sudan: Reflections on the Way Forward"* has made a very useful study of making available the historical heritages and realities which have enriched the South Sudanese throughout the ages. Indeed, the widespread preoccupation with the past in South Sudan, due to a widespread sense of grievance and hurt, underpins the importance of understanding the insights articulated in this book. In the words of George Santanyana, "Progress, far from consisting in change, depends on retentiveness…. Those who cannot remember the past are condemned to repeat it."

A desire to suppress the past can be motivated not only by the desire to avoid pain, or to achieve reconciliation or accommodation with former enemies, but also by a desire to avoid responsibility, shame, and guilt.

Whatever the motivation, burying the past in the sense of suppressing it, is not a reliable strategy, as many elderly war veterans and criminals have discovered late in life. Things that lie buried do not necessarily decompose. Some take root and germinate, then grow only to surface or to be unearthed by former enemies, often when least expected.

This book has posed similar questions in the text: is it fair to ask people to forgive, when regret and remorse have not always been expressed?

And in the long run: will a failure to attend to some of these issues in the present store up problems for the future? The answers are in this book.

This book outlines clearly that there is a convergence of agreement, that in the search for peace, the human person must be the focus. We all know that peace will come to South Sudan, but implementation of the agreement remains the challenge. It may have its shortcomings, but insistence on a gradual process constructing a culture of peace through genuine reconciliation is a wise move.

I congratulate Bishop Eduardo Kussala for this ardent initiative of producing such a valuable resource book, which I regard as a valuable contribution to the promotion of peace and harmony in the world, and particularly in South Sudan. This publishing venture has provided a notable and eminently useful source of information and guidance for people engaged in the ministry of conflict resolution and peace consolidation. May it enjoy the success that it so richly deserves. It proposes hope for the welfare of the people of God.

† Rt. Rev. Joseph Gasi Abangite
Deceased Emeritus Bishop and Father
of the Catholic Diocese of Tombura-Yambio

Prologue

Bakumba and Kumbo, two little brothers, eight and nine years old, were in the kitchen, writing their homework. On the shelf right in front of them was a pot of peanut-paste, half-full.

Bakumba – Hey Kumbo, let's eat some.

Kumbo – We'd rather not, Bakumba. Otherwise, this evening there will not be enough left for the rest of the family; that would not be fair of us and it would make me feel bad.

Bakumba – One spoon each would not make the difference, Kumbo. But if it makes you feel bad, I won't do it either.

Buda, the eldest brother, walked into the kitchen, said nothing, took the peanut-paste, ate all of it and walked out, leaving the others flabbergasted.

Their mother came in to check if they were studying. She saw the empty pot, decided that Bakumba and Kumbo were the culprits, called their father, and had them severely punished. They were tied to the tree for the rest of the day.

Kumbo – Why did Buda not tell Mom he was the one who did it? I love my Mom, but this is not fair. And I hate Buda! He's going to pay for it!

Bakumba – I can see how you feel. But look … it's better for us not to say anything. Okay, so it's not fair. But if we try to discuss things, remember, we're only children, nobody will listen to us, and things are going to grow worse. Let's leave them as they are.

From that day on, Kumbo and Bakumba tried to avoid being alone with Buda and grew suspicious of whatever their big brother would do. The day Buda left for high school they did not even wish him good luck. And for the rest of his life, Buda wondered why.

Nobody ever told him about the drama that changed Kumbo and Bakumba's life that day in the kitchen. If only they had asked him why he did so, the answer would have been so simple: that day Buda felt hungry!

I will never forget this story. It is the story of humankind. If, at best, at times we want to be virtuous, this happens precisely when our neighbour chooses not to be, and vice versa. Thus it becomes easy for both to keep putting the blame on the other. If we don't meet, if we don't sit around a table to open our hearts and discuss matters and admit that we are all responsible for the wrong we've done, there will be no way out, no hope for the future, no future JUSTICE, no future PEACE. The only solution is RECONCILIATION.

RECONCILIATION. That's what this book is all about!

Introduction

South Sudan has been undergoing systematic historical violence during its long journey to freedom. These events have cost South Sudan lives, resources, integrity, human freedom, and above all peace. As a result, a lot of wasted energies have been spent. We are in search of a permanent solution to this issue; hence the theme of reconciliation. Today it has become the most used vocabulary now that the search for peace has become a major goal. People know that a diplomatic resolution to South Sudanese conflicts will not be sufficient to put an end to the war. A deeper process of gradual peace rebuilding is required, which must involve everybody.

The understanding that I wish to offer to the theme of reconciliation for dealing with the South Sudanese tragedy has two main phases. It first of all involves a lot of campaigns, dialogue, negotiations, political and social pressure on the warring parties and every citizen to stop the war or any form of violence. The second perspective of reconciliation concerns a tough and difficult work of restoration – to rebuild a new society once the war is over. This process involves: good leadership; sustained economic and political stability; involvement and collaboration of all citizens; and most importantly, freedom for the victims to acknowledge the failures of the past and for the former oppressors or perpetrators to cooperate.

This reconstruction movement will be time consuming, but it will be a safe and sure means to long-lasting peace in South Sudan. It will take time to heal memories, to invoke oppressors' repentance and for them to ask for forgiveness. It will also take time to begin anew to rearrange those organs of the nation, which, in the past, have caused the violence.

The purpose of writing this book is to encourage all the movements who search for peace – the ones that invoke peace and the ones that need peace – in their move towards a lengthy struggle. It is not my intention, here, to ignore the realities that the victims of these tragedies have been suffering, the worries that have been keeping the people depressed for years. My intention is to take a typical universal Christian approach to understanding reconciliation.

I have divided my work into five chronologically organised chapters. They are designed within the context of South Sudan, and reflect the history of South Sudanese, young and old. This work represents a major effort of thinking in a new way about reconstruction, from the eve of the preparation for independence to the present day's continued violence. It is an attempt to value long-lasting peace reconsiderations. In fact, many specific detailed references typically reflect the situations, times and conflicts in which this work has been written. The prologue at the initial part of this book gives the background to the stories contained herein.

While reading South Sudan's life narrative, and reliving history again, I would like my readers to remember three points. The first is that history must contain the elements of facts and truth. Yes, it is always painful to hear of things that have happened in the past. Therefore, some of the facts I present may be very irritating, but that is history. The second point is that I am South Sudanese, so my interpretation of the situation will be influenced by the reality that I have been living. The third point is that I am also talking about some mistakes that were committed many years ago by people who by now are already dead. Morally there is no genuine reason to condemn an innocent person who never took part in those past offences. The recounting of those errors is meant as a lesson that we should learn from in order to prevent such history from repeating itself.

Reconciliation as such is not an easy subject to write about. Sometimes it is elusive, because at times it tends to seek the wrong thing with the wrong people at the wrong time. This can be seen when considering questions such as: When can, or should, oppressors repent and ask for forgiveness from their victims? Is it possible to embark on reconciliation activities? How can victims and oppressors be brought together?

The many initiatives for peace that have developed on many fronts, both locally and internationally, have prompted me to think about the question of reconciliation, and especially of the deteriorating humanitarian situation in our very young nation.

My first chapter looks at the possibility of reconciliation in the unique context of the South Sudanese story; it considers the actual cases which instigated civil strifes and civil wars, both before and after the birth of independent South Sudan. This is intended to bring to light the more obvious reasons for the conflicts in South Sudan. It is seen as the only way to achieve genuine reconciliation.

The second chapter examines how much the violence in South Sudanese history has cost us. The price of violence has been paid by each and every one of us in various ways, and the only hope for future peace is through reconciliation.

The third chapter looks at how reconciliation can be achieved; it needs the collaboration of all, and the process must be a guided one. The people, victims and all, must be educated so as to work at a permanent reconciliation that will deter future wars. In faith we can stand our ground as responsible Christians or belivers and move towards our brothers and sisters who have sinned against us, in a sincere spirit of personhood and humanity, accepting the human failures of our fellow country men, and moving towards moral reparation.

The fourth chapter looks at the potential of the Church or mosques to use spiritual inspiration drawn from the Word of life and the salvific teaching of God that was simplified through the violent death of Jesus Christ for reconciliation and the salvation of the fallen world.

Much has been discussed about a path towards peace. Much stress has been laid on the role of the Church in the process of reconciliation and in the building of peace in a torn world. If we, as Christians, wish to draw a moral message from our long national tragedy, then it might read as follows: the communal South Sudanese home cannot be assembled by means of economics and politics only. Although these means are the building material without which there is no construction, they are not, however, its foundation.

Finally, in chapter five, and in the conclusion note, the Christian faith possesses abundant means to reinforce reconciliation. Perhaps to some ears this will sound unrealistic, but that does not matter. The gospel as a whole inspires opportunities for peace and communal life, for forgiveness and reconciliation, a good and rich experience of living in a multi-ethnic, multi-religious and multi-cultural ambience in a country like South Sudan.

To find an opportunity to revisit reconciliation in our society after years of persisting conflicts, first of all we should look at the make-up of the country. We must trace, so to speak, the history of this nation that has been sustaining such a lengthy period of violence.

To some readers, to reread the disturbing history of South Sudan might seem unnecessary, and above all unduly provocative, in that it exposes the causes of the pains that this nation has endured.

I agree with some of these feelings, but I feel that true reconciliation should never ignore the causes of the conflicts that have awakened the need for reconciliation. Rather, I would like to use reconciliation as an instrument of peace. Here the basic principle is to remember and not to forget the causes of pain.

To try and forget the pain or the violence caused to us would be quite dangerous and, if generated by fear, it would psychologically destroy the evidence in us. That is, we would be forcing ourselves to forget a specific part of ourselves, and so, to lose our real selves. There is no way to escape that, but there seems to be no way to accept it either.

My approach is pastoral. I deal with how to motivate the entire population of South Sudan to live out, in practice, the Gospel of peace as preached by Christ and guided by the Church's doctrine on peace, to help them grow into fuller Christians, for a life of true dignity.

I think that the past is not dead and gone, it is not even past. This is very true for people who have lost their fortunes. When people become unsuccessful, they immediately become the bearers of the longest memories of historic pain. In this case many of us have sustained long memories indeed.

The only way forward for such people is to make their way through it. They can succeed in unloading much of their long memories in their community. The community of human persons is alive because of the shared understanding of people who make up part of that community. Thus, without a culture of mutual understanding, the human family breaks into fragments.

A second way for these injured people to walk out of their long memories is through the good hands of their government. The government has to assume responsibility of the painful past, especially if the pain that people suffered was caused by the country's political or military leadership. Victims need the justice that they were denied in the past to be demonstrated in the present and in the future.

With this in mind, I believe that we should trace back the antecedent to the reality of today, before we can genuinely think of reaching true reconciliation in a nation like South Sudan, which has spent a lifetime in violence. In fact, the target of this book remains: to seek deliverance from the yoke of violence.

Meaningful reconciliation and permanent peace can flourish in our country only if we will be able to identify the reasons for today's conflict and above all, if we will get to know one another more intimately through various interactions.

MAP OF THE REPUBLIC OF SOUTH SUDAN

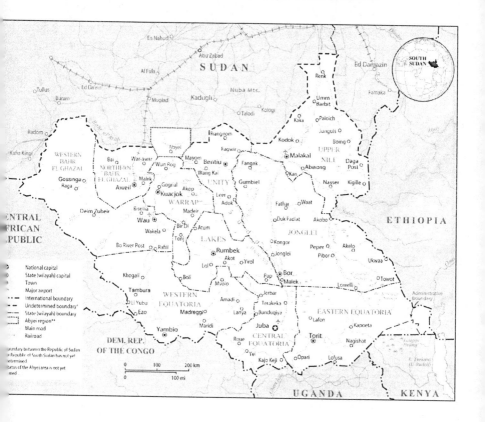

CHAPTER ONE

How Much Our Conflicts Cost Us

South Sudan at the Crossroads of Violence

The definition of war by Alexander Berkman reveals exactly how war, over the decades, has defamed our image as a nation:

> "War paralyses your courage and deadens the spirit of true manhood, that 'tis not yours to think and reason why, but to do and die like the hundred thousand others doomed like yourself. War means blind obedience, unthinking stupidity, brutish callousness, wanton destruction, and irresponsible murder."[1]

This chapter speaks aloud about the impact of the violence that we have endured during this and other civil troubles. Its words sound painful as they tell about the reality that war and violence can produce. The responsibility lies in the hands of the government and at every South Sudanese. Its leadership must take the primary responsiblity, since leaders are supposed to guide the entire nation in peace. By mentioning the weaknesses of the government, the chapter does not intend to ignore the good that the government has done; rather, it encourages the government to assume a broad responsibility for peace and for the development of all.

The patriotic elders and patrons of South Sudan's independence worked hard to achieve and hand over to us the 'South Sudan liberated'. All the well-intentioned South Sudanese treasured the hope that South Sudan would become a free and democratic new republic, sovereign, secular, guaranteeing all South Sudanese people social justice, and economic and political equality. Opportunity would reign, fraternity among all would be promoted, a country where, in spite of differences, the dignity of individuals and the unity and integrity of the nation would be assured.

The long and festering civil strife in South Sudan that had already begun to appear before independence has generated absolute poverty, tangible

---

[1] "Warisstupid.com" website, http://www.hickorytech.net/warisstupid/ page2/, downloaded on 14/03/2004.

through hunger, war and escalating suffering. The results are disastrous for the ordinary people who are left in the depths of poverty, with practically no way to organise themselves.[2] As a result, thousands of us today live as refugees in permanent poverty, far from our homelands. Millions of others live as internally displaced persons (IDPs) in a very degrading and painful situation. This was best described by Sudanese bishops in their pastoral letter '*Blessed Are the Peace-Makers*' of 1993:

> War of its very nature, is evil. War is unworthy of human beings. Those statements need no arguments to support them. One has only to look at what is happening to our country because of the civil war. Whole towns and villages have been devastated or completely destroyed, thus putting an end to the sacrifices, the labour and the wealth of several generations of South Sudanese. Thousands and thousands of people – *human beings* – have been killed, among them women and children killed in cold blood. No party to the war can escape the guilt of such mass and indiscriminate murders. Hundreds of thousands of others have been displaced by the war, reduced to poverty and real misery, and rendered homeless and unwelcome wherever they go. All over the country sections of the population are deliberately incited to hate, to maltreat and even kill those who do not belong to their group.... Yet the psychosis of war has prevented us from understanding that war is the single major cause of this impoverishment. We need to ask ourselves a challenging question: Who is going to help us reconstruct what we have so wantonly destroyed?[3]

If things continue, in another century from now the people of South Sudan will still continue to have the highest percentage of illiterate people. As South Sudan is today, the majority of South Sudanese have never been fully incorporated into well-guided educational methods for children. The more illiterate our population remains, the more unemployment and underdevelopment will persist in our nation, and there will continue to be glaring differences in people's ability to feed, clothe and house themselves. Are we destined to have more hideous banditries of underworld crime and criminals and barefoot, illiterate children, a corrupt government, organised crimes, killings and recurring wars?

In 1992, Archbishop Gabriel Zubeir (now Cardinal), decided that the major seminarians were to be involved in pastoral activities in the parishes

---

[2]   Cf. UNDP 2004 Report, World Resources Institute, World Resources 2003-2004, p. 116.
[3]   South Sudanese Catholic Bishops' affirmation in their pastoral letter "Blessed Are the Peace Makers, A Call to Reconciliation and Peace, § 1", in *Letters to the Church of South Sudan*, Sudan Catholic Bishops' Conference, Khartoum 2000, p. 147.

and centres of the Archdiocese of Khartoum (Republic of Sudan). I was sent to work among displaced South Sudanese in Jebel Aulia, together with three colleagues. We were merely seminarians under formation. Lazarus Mundua came from Yei, William Chan Acuil from Wau, John Bosco Dindo from Juba and I was from Tombura-Yambio. At that stage, I was attending the senior class (year three of Theology). The displaced South Sudanese that we were to serve had been dumped in the open desert by the government, about 18 miles away from the capital, Khartoum. In this camp, there were about 75,000 people who were living in a true state of poverty and destitution. They lacked almost all basic necessities, they had no jobs, and they had to depend on the little food donations given by charitable organisations and Churches.

Most sad to see were the children, especially the underaged. During the dry cold winter, mothers had to make holes in the ground to try to keep their kids warm. Since we had pitched our tents right in the middle of the camp, we played a notable role in animation and reconciling conflicts. The displaced people came from different ethnic groups from the South, and some groups had never lived together before. In this situation, we had a number of problems to solve.

It is quite true that a high rate of poverty breeds violence. Displaced, and in the middle of the desert, the people in the camp were questioning the notion of justice. The younger ones, having nothing to keep them busy, were being forced into violence of all kinds. They loved to listen and sing one of Bob Marley's songs,[4] *"War,"* which seemed to refer to their own situation. The hardest thing to do was to explain or define the word justice to the displaced people in the camp. Bob Marley's song was like an anthem.

---

[4]   Taken from Bob Marley's Album.

War

Until the philosophy which holds one race
Superior and another inferior
Is finally and permanently discredited and abandoned
Everywhere is war, me say war

That until there is no longer first class
And second class citizens of any nation
Until the colour of a man's skin
Is of no more significance than the colour of his eyes
Me say war

That until the basic human rights are equally
Guaranteed to all, without regard to race
Dis a war

We were principally sent to these camps to help in the pastoral and spiritual animation of the displaced people during our three months with them, but at the end of the day we found ourselves involved in activities that were more social than spiritual. The fact that the four of us were coming from different ethnic groups helped very much in the reconciliation process, since we were able to speak most of the major languages of the people in the camps.

Conflicts and wars have prevented South Sudan from growing economically. The nation is blessed with enormous reserves of natural resources, oil, gold, copper, etc., yet it ranks low among the 173 less developed countries according to the U.N. Human Development Reports. This is not a surprise since for more than half of her history, and continuing into the country's freedom, South Sudan has been living in violence.

Among the many problems and crises that have befallen South Sudan, there is the impact of nepotism, tribalism, and communalism. These practices have become bones of contention among the people. More explicitly, no aspect of our life has been spared some negative impact, whether coming from ethnic radicalism or regionalism influences. The real concern is that our mentality and consciousness is being guided by some sort of fanaticism, which at times the powerful elite will call patriotism.

South Sudan, with all its beauty and its privilege of being the newest or the Benjamin of the world, incredibly has now become famous for persisting civil wars. Is it ethically correct to allow for our poor and innocent people to be paid back in kind today for the past mistakes that have become South Sudan's history? Who is so powerful that he can enshrine God into one small spot, or force him to belong to one specific group only? How much longer should we permit political criminality to occur, committed by us, thus perpetuating violence? How can people be sensitised about the natural interdependence of human persons? But why and how did we arrive at such an extreme degradation?

The truth of the matter is that we, South Sudanese, are to blame for the brutality that accompanies our daily life. We have been terribly mishandled, cheated and exploited by foreigners and continue to be blackmailed by our own people. But, regrettably, we are also truly victims of our own moral and psychological weaknesses.

And what is very worrying is that the crises have sunk deep into everybody. The majority of the people who support or implement the will of our leaders are illiterate, and misinformed masses that are not aware of the real affairs of our country. On the other hand, many of the educated and well-informed South Sudanese have become bystanders and are reluctant to actively participate because of their complacency and indifference. Some are made to fight and defend "the cause" with their life. Jesus spoke against such a situation in defence of the truth when he said, "You know that those who are recognised as rulers over the Gentiles lord it over them. And their great ones make their authority over them felt. But it shall not be so among you. Rather whoever wishes to be great among you will be your servant" (Mark 10:42-43). The Lord Jesus wanted the attitude of everybody towards one another to be an attitude of service. The absence of this value is what is causing problems and poverty.

Poverty, the Biting Beast

Before and after the independence of South Sudan, the neglect of the poor has continued unabated, without a sustainable solution, fuelled by conflicts and the violence of war.

Poverty is the inability to own the basic necessities for survival, namely for safety and security. This understanding of poverty is correct and shared equally by the UNDP (United Nations Development Programme):

> A key dimension of human poverty is known as human security. This concept is introduced in the 1994 Human Development Report. It means that people can exercise their choices safely and freely, confident that they will not lose in the future the opportunities that they have today. Human security has two main aspects: safety from such chronic threats as hunger, disease and repression and protection from sudden and hurtful shocks in the pattern of life.[5]

In fact, the African definition of poverty in some instances is completely different and unique. The African perception of poverty goes beyond the absence of material possession. Poverty is not understood in relation with wealth or richness. Wealth or richness in the African tradition is measured in relation to the abundance of life lived in relations, namely with the Supreme Being, the Spirits, ancestors, fellow human beings and the rest of creation. Poverty is the lack of abundance of life and the absence of proper relationships.[6]

For centuries, the poor in this country have been caught up in a vicious cycle and have remained poor, bearing the brunt of poverty even to the extent of hunger and starvation.

Elements that are visible signs of South Sudanese poverty are these: malnutrition, low or no income, low consumption and expenditure, chronic illness, illiteracy, unemployment, unhygienic living conditions. These ills are endured by people in various ways.

In the midst of the agony of the poor people, several elite people have built heaven for themselves at the expense of the powerless. The elite speak of development, modernisation, self-sufficiency and growth. But we all know that development means being able to freely decide one's destiny. Development must include making choices about the quality of life one wishes to attain. Now, very much so, poverty is a lack of choice. In Source-Yubu, in 1984 a power generator was unloaded in the centre of the town, and it brought joy to many. I did not know where it came from, nor did many others, until my father one evening explained to us the dirty tricks that surrounded it. He told us not to be moved by its presence. It was believed that the Sudanese and Egyptian governments had refused to

---

[5]   UNDP, Human Development Report 1999, (Oxford University Press, 1999, p. 38).
[6]   From an interview with Benedict Ssettuma (from Massaka Diocese, Uganda) one of the aspiring and dynamic young African theologians, Rome, 2nd November 2004.

grant approval to the Southern Sudanese's request to build a hydroelectric power station at Nimule on the River Nile, which would have supplied the whole of South Sudan with electric power. Instead, a hundred of these generators were distributed all over the southern towns and villages, without equipping them with the necessary accessories, just to keep the people quiet and buy time. These generators can still be found today and they have never been put into action. When you do not have choices, you are poor. And when the poor are forced to do risky jobs, such as engaging in military service for the wrong reason, or they have no education, no house, no health security, no land, they have absolutely no choice.

The estimated 4.2 million South Sudanese who died before and after independence were mainly illiterate and marginalised people. Their story is horrible to hear, and tells about starving people waiting for help, attention, death or slavery, whichever came first. All of them were victims of human neglect, of violence that has no human pity.

In every human society there are problems regarding inter-relationships. The case of South Sudan is no exception to this historical and social phenomenon. If we consider poverty as a social phenomenon, the causes of poverty in our beloved nation need to be identified with the help of scientific analysis of the existing socio-economic system.

To poor people, who have no say in the distribution of available resources, in the government's development schemes or in the military service that concerns their own lives, economic freedom is an empty dream, political freedom is an absurdity, and life in general remains a perennial and painful struggle.

The Symposium of the Episcopal Conferences of Africa and Madagascar (SECAM) gives a summary of the African conflict thus:

> A careful look at these conflicts in Africa and in the world creates a feeling of panic and helplessness. One gets the impression that the forces of evil and death grip every part of the human community, and worse still, that our chances of emerging from this cycle of violence, armed conflict, and war, are practically non-existent.[7]

Hunger, disease, ignorance and superstition have pushed a great nation to the bottom of the list of developing nations. Of course, a country's poverty is expressed in terms of poor resources and low national income,

---

SECAM, Pastoral Letter, "Christ Our Peace" (Eph 2:14)": The Church-as-Family of God, Place and Sacrament of Pardon, Reconciliation and Peace in Africa, SECAM Publications, Kumasi Catholic Press Ltd., October 2001, p. 42.

yet more money easily makes its way into sponsoring the civil war which continues to destroy poor people. The result is a low per capita income, high disparity in income distribution, and so on.

In South Sudan, it is poor and inefficient utilisation of resources, rampant corruption and considerable mismanagement of resources at political and bureaucratic levels, and above all, lack of collective national will that have resulted in poverty and underdevelopment becoming endemic. It is our contention that all the sufferings of the masses are the result of long persisting civil wars. But a major problem remains the short-sightedness of South Sudanese people, and their failure to see and treat each other as equal human beings.

The Fate of the Vulnerable

The rule of violence that pervades our country could be lessened if children were taught love instead of violence, peace instead of war, reconciliation instead of revenge. Let me tell the story of an episode that happened in Khartoum. I was travelling from Khartoum North to Ommdurman in a public bus. On this bus, there happened to be two women who sat opposite each other. One of the women, an Arab, was carrying her one-year-old baby, and the other woman was a black African South Sudanese. The Arab child started to smile, pushing its little arms out towards the black woman, but the mother tried to divert its attention away. The more she insisted on diverting its attention away from the African woman, the more the child screamed and cried. This is when the African woman intervened and said to the Arab woman "*Ya Hagia* (respectful title for married women) give me the child to carry, because this child does not know yet how much you Arab Sudanese hate us South Sudanese or how much we South Sudanese hate you Arabs; it is still an angel." As the Arab woman finally surrendered the baby boy into the arms of the black woman, the child was at peace, laughed, and ended up sleeping. Women have a natural capacity for making peace. The child created an opportunity for dialogue and interpersonal relationship.

Children

For decades, millions of children in South Sudan have been living in hard-working conditions. Military service ranks high among all, followed by house enslavement. Some working children are between the age of 7-14 years old, and work several hours a day. Everybody feels and knows that children are our future. They are our assets and resources. But as a nation we lack very much a genuine programme for our children, especially for poor children.

Jesus, aware of their innocence of life, calls the children blameless; as such they are promised inheritance of the kingdom of heaven: "Let the little children come to me; do not stop them, for it is to such as these that the kingdom of God belongs" (Mark 10:14-15). When the government of the people is missing, the result is nothing but uncertainty and disorder.

Women, the elderly, and other weak individuals

Women, as first teachers, medical persons, and economists of families, can make peace reign in a society because of their abundant love. Women have natural talents for creating an atmosphere of love and joy. However, South Sudanese women are faced with enormous problems. The low value placed on female life is the biggest problem. Women suffer malnutrition, lack of medical attention, early marriage and frequent childbirths.

John Paul II affirms the societal obligation to take care of women:

> Experience confirms that there must be a *social re-evaluation of the mother's role,* of the toil connected with it, and of the need that children have for care, love and affection in order that they may develop into responsible, morally and religiously mature and psychologically stable persons. It will redound to the credit of society to make it possible for a mother, without inhibiting her freedom, without psychological or practical discrimination … to devote herself to taking care of her children and educating them in accordance with their needs, which vary with age.[8]

South Sudanese women are in most instances, if not always, undervalued. This results in categorising women as primarily domestic workers and therefore only as supplementary earners in society. In many cases, employment of women is restricted to a few select sectors and they are given no opportunity in the so-called male-dominated spheres just because they are women. Deprivation of equal wages for equal work and lack of maternity benefits are the order of the day.

Looking at South Sudan's general situation, the marginalisation of women in developmental processes and an oppressive social reality highlight the miserable plight of women and the long struggle that lies ahead of them. It is beyond doubt that, as far as the gender relations existing in our society are concerned, women's contribution has not been

---

JOHN PAUL II, Encyclical *Laborem Exercens,* n. 19.

recognised fully, and women are not adequately acknowledged as active partners in developmental activities. The potential of women has been largely ignored.

Women must be given a greater share in decision-making and in programme implementation. This can be achieved through a greater representation of women in local administration, political parties, state assemblies and the parliament.

What South Sudan needs is an awareness of inequality, and a conscious will to fight discrimination as a precondition for social change. Sustained activity by women's groups has been instrumental in generating social awareness about women's problems. At some point in their lives, women are forced to re-examine their relationships with others, especially men. This reassessment, usually with the help of some social support, leads to a new awareness and a commitment to know more about themselves. One of the indispensable challenges is to foster and nurture such social supports to help women reassess their personalities and to become more aware of the inequalities and oppression existing in our system.

With women the process of social development and peace construction can grow very rapidly. And above all, in our situation of conflict and need for reconciliation, peace can more easily be attained through women, who are indeed symbols of peace.

A Call to Good Governance

Democratic practices will animate and unite each and every member of society, regardless of his/her social background, to participate in directing the country. Democracy will enable each member, even the lowest one in the country, to climb up and guide others.

Pope John Paul II stresses it thus:

> The Church values the democratic system inasmuch as it ensures the participation of citizens in making political choices, guarantees to the governed the possibility both of electing and holding accountable those who govern them, and of replacing them through peaceful means when appropriate. Thus she cannot encourage the formation of narrow ruling groups which usurp the power of the State for individual interests or for ideological ends. Authentic democracy is possible only in a State ruled by law, and on the basis of a correct conception of the human person.[9]

---

[9]   ID., Encyclical *Centesimus Annus*, n. 46.

One of the main failures is the use of leadership and political careers for the promotion of individual and personal gain.

Today, around the world, education has been accepted as an essential foundation for a culture of good governance through democratic procedures, but in South Sudan the education system is a sad story. The importance of imparting knowledge to the people as a means of securing and protecting liberty can never be over emphasised. For democracy to be achieved, literacy is the first step.

Instead of developing sobriety, national unity, understanding and a sense of nationalism, certain elements of our education have cultivated hunger for power, hatred, ethnicity, nepotism, divisiveness, unfair competition and unhealthy attitudes among the people as a whole. The South Sudanese Catholic Bishops have left no stone unturned in their attempts to enlighten both the government and the people to find proper ways and means for ruling South Sudan. In their pastoral letter *"Blessed Are the Peace-Makers"*, calling for reconciliation and peace, they expressed themselves thus:

> Work therefore for peace. The war will end only if we are prepared to lay down our arms, and to curb in ourselves whatever contributes to war.... Peace is more than the absence of war. A civil war in particular grows out of situations of injustice; the denial or the suppression of legitimate rights and freedoms, the unequal distribution of resources and opportunities people need for their advancement, and all types of discrimination.... To this list we must add: the scarcity of essential commodities; poor and insufficient administration; the harassment of the citizens by security persons and others who do so for their own interests; the poor administration of justice, and the practice, whether official or otherwise, of favouring people according to their tribes, race or religion.[10]

Religion, Too, Can Be Violent

It is to be hoped that the religious background of the people of South Sudan could contribute to creating peaceful coexistence between the children of this land, between Traditionals, Christians and Muslims. There is no doubt that the past history of South Sudan had been full of religious violence and intolerance. Religious convictions did speed and influence the process of independence. But after independence, and until this very day, South Sudan has been swimming in a stream of blood caused by lack of respect for others.

---

[10]   South Sudanese Catholic Bishops' Pastoral Letter, "Blessed Are the Peace Makers" § 3, op. cit., p. 149.

It is possible for some who came from South Sudan before independence to conclude that religions have done less good in the country, and rather caused more bloodshed. However, before drawing a conclusion it will be useful to seriously examine the purpose of religion. Religion is not limited only to religious celebrations. It is neither a political ideology nor a cultural practice. It is much nobler than all these. Religion is the harbinger of unity, an agent of peace and harmony, the promoter of genuine love among human beings, a source of support in different types of human experiences, a means to lead a human being to God and an instrument that can help human beings to discover the inner depth of reality. In short, the purpose of religion is to establish a close link between man and God and a harmonious relationship among human beings.

When we look at religion from these perspectives, there is no doubt that religion and religious values are necessary for life. These values have been guiding the life of all societies and continue to guide today's societies and communities. Religion and religious values are essential for social life and social relationships.

Sadly, some religions or individuals have to some degree degraded themselves and have lost their focus, moving away from the very purpose for which they had come into existence. Religions have been subverted in the hands of some of the religious leaders that have wanted to exercise control and power over their followers. They have also been used to frighten people with all kinds of mysterious, superstitious and mythological practices and utterances. Religion has been used by different sections of society to suit their own needs. Some church preachers have misused the opportunity of bringing people back to their God by alienating them with poor or unhealthy spiritual homilies. They have targeted public figures in their sermons, which has caused huge scandals among many church-goers. Others have used religion to acquire or exercise political leverage, and businessmen have used it to gain monetary benefits.

Therefore, because of these developments and many others in history, the role of religion is being questioned by the modern generations who no longer see the need for such a structure or organisation. Pope John Paul II, in an address upon his arrival in Sudanese capital Khartoum back in 1992, encouraged Sudanese, as followers of God, to work for the good of all:

> I have kissed the soil of Sudan with profound sentiments of peace and goodwill. I give thanks to Almighty God who has led my pilgrim steps to this land, and gives me the opportunity to speak on behalf of understanding, harmony and peace among believers who, though they follow different traditions, never-

theless honour God in their hearts and seek to do his will in all things.... I make this ardent appeal to you: let us listen to the voice of our brothers and sisters, especially those oppressed by poverty, hunger and violence, as they cry out for justice and peace, and for a new era of dialogue and agreement.[11]

As young priests back in 1994, my colleague Fr Paul Sebit Okum and I were celebrating Holy Mass in one of the shanty towns called Soba, south of Khartoum International Airport. We suddenly noticed the Christians rushing off from the prayer shelter with their hands closed on their noses while children were screaming. When I looked at Fr Paul, he was already off. I was confused and could not understand what was happening. Finally I felt something chilly in my nose too. I realised it was caused by smoking guns or tear gas, which was being shot in our direction, just to disrupt our prayer service. The Christians, after the prayers, were very angry because of this offence and were ready to react until we pleaded with them to calm down. Later, when we went to ask the police officer in charge of the area what had happened, we were told that the police did not aim at us; the wind blew in our direction. "Who then were the police shooting at?" was our question. There was no answer to that. This is one of the behaviours that generate hatred. It shows how people are being pushed into evil actions, and how violence can be fuelled.

In a country like ours, one important task that any genuine religious leader should think about is to promote love for humanity, human rights, reconciliation, healing, hard work, and peace through ongoing dialogue. Such dialogue should not aim at debating against one another or discrediting each other. It should be a constructive effort through which the positive aspects of every individual, institution or religion can be identified and promoted. This will create a sense of respect and acceptance and will also promote a better understanding among the multi-cultural and multi-ethnic society. Serious study and reflection on religious matters will be particularly useful in schools and colleges where young minds can be exposed to different religions and helped to understand and accept one another without discrimination.

Conversion of individual believers from one religion to another should never be a bone of contention in South Sudan, as it was once in the Sudan of the past. According to the Human Rights Declaration,

---

[11] Opening speech of His Holiness, during his visit to South Sudan at the Welcoming Ceremony, February 10th 1993, in *Letters to the Church of South Sudan,* Sudan Catholic Bishops' Conference, Khartoum 2000, p. 254, § 1.

"In principle, every person has the right to choose the religion of his own choice, depending on his convictions and perceptions. No one can prevent a person from exercising this right. At the same time, no one has the right to compel anyone either to embrace a particular religion or to abandon it."[12]

The time has come for the believers to realise that in South Sudan, while many religious and ethnic groups are becoming more conscious about their rights, it is necessary for them to give up all aggressiveness and instead opt for peaceful coexistence.

Jesus Christ, the Son of God, in his Sermon on the Mount, and also by his many examples, teaches that "There is no greater love than to lay down one's life for one's friends" (John 15:13). This clearly means that one should be prepared to die for one's friends, but should never be ready to kill. Jesus stands as a model for all believers who seek peace. Yes, there is hope. If we have problems, or if we fail, we must acknowledge it and turn towards God for forgiveness. The following chapter will tell us more as to how to overcome the state of violence and attain peace.

Summary

"South Sudan at the crossroads of violence" is a very good description of our nation since her conception. Throughout her modern history, she has been bathing in the blood of her own people due to violence of all kinds. This violence has cost the country many things: lives, sovereignty, respect, and prosperity, and, above all, peace. South Sudan has become the object of sympathy and cheap propaganda by many, in various ways.

This situation has had a major impact on the whole land and the result is disastrous. It will take time to put things right. South Sudanese feel humiliated by their own people. No answers are at hand and people feel confused. The hopes and visions of ordinary individuals have become null and void.

Poverty has taken possession of the country in all its spheres and its pinch is very much felt by ordinary men and women. The most essential things for living and growing are always beyond their reach. Poverty has done nothing but ignite violence among people in South Sudan.

Without doubt, the burden and cost of this are being carried by the most vulnerable in the society – children and women. Children grow up

---

[12] Henry I. STEINER and Philip ALSTON, International Human Rights in Context: Law, Politics and Morals, Oxford University Press, 2000, p. 469.

learning nothing but killing and warring, hatred and revenge, tribalism and nepotism, etc. Women, who play a greater role in the growth and development of a nation, are sidelined and abused. This is despite the fact that, in reality, 80% of the sustainable effort to keep South Sudanese people alive is being provided by women. As men engage in warfare, women are left alone to fend for their children, the soldiers, and themselves. As Abraham Flexner says:

> "Nations, have recently been led to borrow billions for war; but no nation has ever been able to borrow largely for education. Probably, no nation is rich enough to pay for both war and civilisation. We must make our choice; we cannot have both."[13]

As South Sudanese and people of one nation, we need to find new techniques: first and foremost, community dialogue, forgiveness, compromise, solidarity in action, respect and compassion. These are needed to bring our country back to her original destiny of peace and prosperity.

This chapter has said much about the damage caused by the conflicts in South Sudan. The following chapter will, instead, dwell on how to educate ourselves to accept the past and build a peaceful future.

---

[13] "Warisstupid.com" website, http://www.hickorytech.net/warisstupid/ page2/, downloaded on 14/03/2004Ibid

Questions for Reflection

1. What are most visible and serious impacts that the ongoing violence has had on South Sudan?

2. One of the prominent South Sudanese, Dominique Kassiano, once said, "War is Development." Can you think of any positive impact of the prolonged history of violence in South Sudan?

3. Do you think the current problems and difficulties that South Sudan is now experiencing are necessarily part and parcel of the mistakes which are said to have been committed in the past?

4. Is it possible to identify which group in society is bearing the brunt of the impact of the ongoing violence? Similarly, is it possible to identify which group in society has benefited the most from the violence?

5. Is there any way to arrest or reverse the present social and political violence once and forever?

6. Can we re-energise and revitalise ourselves and act together, as people of goodwill, for a common cause, despite our different social backgrounds?

7. The cost of our conflicts will continue to increase unless we all can decide to pursue peace. To achieve a positive conclusion requires a lot more. What are some examples of what it would require?

8. Many nations in the world have suffered wars and destruction but they later reconciled. Can we reconcile?

CHAPTER TWO

Reconciliation
Is the Responsibility of All

Violence Can Be Halted

With foresight, one can optimistically say that one day South Sudan will move towards the road to permanent peace. However, the question is *how* and *when*, and, above all, *who* is going to steer the country to that place, and how is the war going to stop? Keen observers can notice that South Sudan has been struggling to come up with solutions for the vast political, economic, social, and ethnic problems that have beset it for centuries. The pastoral letter of South Sudanese Bishops, *"Do Not Let Evil Defeat You,"* published in 1989, called on the people to seek ways and means to end the violence:

> Perhaps the greatest challenge is the call for all of us to examine our own lives, to identify how we can choose generosity over selfishness, and choose a real commitment to family and community over individual acquisition and ambition. In many small ways, each of us can help overcome violence by dealing with it on our block, providing for the emotional, physical, and spiritual needs of our children, dealing with our own abusive behaviour. Believe in the power of love. It is the power of Christ.... Love and forgiveness are not virtues of cowards, but of men and women of strong will and in our case, of strong convictions.[14]

Violence is overcome day-by-day, choice-by-choice, and person-by-person. All of us must make a contribution. The question, more desperately echoed than ever before, is: Will South Sudan be consumed by its past or will it finally fulfil its vast potential and become a peaceful, modern and vibrant nation? What is beyond doubt right now, however, is that the situation at the present time is very serious and dangerous.

Sudan Catholic Bishops' Conference, Letters to the Church of South Sudan, Khartoum 2000, pp. 178 179

Can we identify who can be blamed for our problems and failures? Both the administrators and the politicians blame each other for being at the root of the problem. The Christians blame the Muslims and the Muslims blame the Christians, the non-believers blame the so-called believers in God, and vice versa. It would greatly help if the two arms of government were to accept responsibility for the damage that their conduct, throughout the ages, has unleashed upon our nation. Has nobody ever told them about the law and its consequences? If they were to combine their considerable talents and energies and use the vast resources of government machinery and funds effectively, and in accordance with the dictates found in the Scriptures, it would greatly help in taking this nation towards greater stability and prosperity.

The educated classes automatically tend to blame the government for the ills of the country and to see themselves as victims of a callous environment. It seems, therefore, a treachery to whisper aloud that this wringing of hands by the educated classes and their own behaviour and abdication of individual responsibility are major hindrances to crucial development.

It is more appropriate to admit that all of us South Sudanese are responsible for our crises. However awful and unwelcome it may be, the inescapable must be acknowledged: we must all accept our share of responsibility for bringing about change. It will, of course, demand a lot of sacrifices and a purification of our consciences. A lot of prudence is needed in tackling this complicated problem of South Sudan.

South Sudanese people must be involved in how and what to do for their country. Difficult as it may seem to accept, there are no such things as societal attitudes and cultures. There are only individual attitudes, which together make up commonly accepted attitudes. Unsurprisingly, people who live in close proximity to each other display similar attitudes. What is required is that each individual should take responsibility for his own behaviour. Being an example to others is what is called for. The rest will follow.

In the long term, the only way forward is to create a population that is not susceptible to manipulation. Only education can equip people to see this. Constant dwelling on past grievances can only give rise to a vicious cycle of revenge. We can only go back into our history to learn from our errors and successes in order to build a peaceful future.

Naturally, there are risks and sacrifices involved for those who wish to be catalysts of change. History is replete with examples of people who suffered indignities, violence, loss of livelihood and worse for standing up against falsehood and insisting on the truth.

South Sudan loves heroes. Sadly, we tend not to be too demanding or discriminating about the qualities or qualifications that we want our heroes to have. Before anything else, we need to re-appraise our own role and responsibility. Fear should be replaced by courage and this needs religious values. We cannot change people, but people can be moulded. Yes, the current conflicts can be halted if the Sermon on the Mount of Jesus can penetrate the hearts of people. Blessed are those who mourn, blessed are the meek, those who hunger for justice; blessed are the merciful and the pure in heart, the peacemakers (*Matthew* 5:3-10). This is the great teaching of Jesus urgently needed by South Sudanese society today.

Education Enhances Social Transformation

Poverty is South Sudan's major problem today. The disintegrating situation we are witnessing now is only an aberration of what the great South Sudan could be: a witness of unity in diversity. After independence, we all hoped and wanted to turn our attention to eradicating poverty. But the problems accumulated over centuries could not be resolved in a short span of time. And only a few months later, we had to raise guns against our own people again, guns which have not yet gone silent. The task of leading South Sudan should have been handed over to our country's educated minority, with a sense of sacrifice, social concern and dedication. Rather, the nation seems to have hoped in vain.

The tools provided by a sound education would greatly improve people's chances of carving out a decent livelihood, yet such opportunities are just not available to them. This situation has spurred me to make greater use of the prayer for serenity, which is very fitting for difficult cases: *God grant me the courage to change the things I can, the patience to accept the things I can't, and the wisdom to know the difference.*

All presidents in the world, during their election campaigns, promise their electorates that, if elected, they will improve the lives of the people through education, because education opens the flood gates of knowledge, providing the tools for developing one's innate skills, which in turn lead to the chance of economic emancipation and, in a fuller sense, to spiritual emancipation. Thus, one can see that the education of our masses is a fundamental necessity and should be at the root of all developmental activity.

In South Sudan, the development of the individual has received a very low priority in our planning process so far. Education, which can dismantle all barriers of regionalism, redundancy, corruption and ethnic violence, has all along been relegated to an insignificant corner, in large part because of the prolonged and ongoing conflict. Vast swathes of the South Sudanese population have been left behind in education. The few schools that exist outside the state capitals do not have proper buildings, blackboards, furniture, stationery, and, most importantly of all, well trained and motivated teachers. Primary school teachers should be well-trained men and women with a strong nationalistic spirit.

The purpose of education is not simply to teach the three R's (reading, writing and arithmetic), but is also to enable the individual to develop his or her potential and to develop a strong individual character. The challenge, therefore, is how to bring about a resurgence of the national spirit and build up a strong individual character, and thereby a strong national character, for the good of the country. Strength of character is not necessarily an innate quality. It can be cultivated by proper education and by a good family background. The younger generation needs to be inculcated with the right kind of value. They should be taught that our happiness relies on the happiness of others, that discipline leads to progress, and so on. The reversal of the present trend and the strengthening of the moral fibre of the nation should start with schools; our schools and colleges should impart a proper sense of values.

The women of South Sudan have an important role to play in this regard. They can wield great influence over young minds and instill in them a sense of pride in our culture and heritage, a spirit of sacrifice and selfless service, and compassion for fellow beings. The qualities that a good citizen should possess are those that can engage in building a platform to peace. But what if the woman herself is illiterate?

With certainty, a great responsibility lies on the shoulders of our teachers, especially in primary, middle and high schools, where the process of character building takes place. A responsible teaching community can help develop a strong national character, without which no nation can survive or progress. Here much should be said to the credit of the South Sudanese Catholic Bishops' Conference, which, through individual bishops in their respective dioceses, for years has maintained the greater part of educational infrastructures everywhere in South Sudan. Despite the damage of the on-going civil wars, they have been silently doing this job of character building without any fanfare or publicity.

Rosemary Ruether explains the role of Jesus in helping the masses of Israel awake to the reality of their rights. She says:

We are led to recognition of Jesus as the iconoclastic prophet who chastised the existing social and religious hierarchies for lording their power over those subject to them. In doing this ... Jesus sought to reverse the (existing) social order, making empowerment and the liberation of the oppressed the meaning of servanthood ... Jesus tried to teach that right relationship with God rejects a dominant-subordinate model in which the relationship between God and human beings is used to justify any type of oppression.[15]

Reconstruction Needs the Hands of All Citizens

The only way forward is to give up hatred and revenge, then join hands to rid our country of all vices by giving it the taste of peace. South Sudan has indeed been mishandled and mismanaged. Since a country is not just a geo-political entity, but consists of people, the traitors are the people themselves. During their struggle for independence, the people of South Sudan came to believe, as did many other European colonies, that the achievement of political freedom would automatically bring with it a prosperity they had not known previously. An initial period of euphoria followed independence, but this joy quickly came to an end when it became apparent that successive colonisations had left the nation fragmented and the land almost drained of its resources. Nevertheless, all the many right-minded people of South Sudan must not now fall into panic and despair. They must be prepared, with some degree of international assistance, to make a determined effort to halt the country's present decline into chaos.

Many of us after July 9th 2011 sat back to enjoy the fruits of freedom, leaving the governance to a handful of people with complex past tales. Many evils were tolerated during this period; avoiding them would have prevented the current armed conflict. Our freedom soon became an illusion. Now we have a long struggle on our hands.

Effective development cannot be brought about by a few scholars or by an ethnic group. Real change takes place at ground level. We cannot, therefore, in the field of education, be content merely with providing the means for high academic achievement amongst an elite minority. It is essential, also, to provide basic elementary education for all children of the coming generation and to enable as many young people as possible to acquire practical skills and technical know-how. If people could, for example, maintain and repair their own transport vehicles and electric-

---

[15] Rosemary Ruether's observation is referred to in MARY HEMBROW SNYDER, *The Christology of Rosemary Radford Ruether,* Mystic, CT: Twenty-Third Publications, 1988, p. 68.

ity generators, dig their own wells and set up their own simple irriga-
tion schemes, much would be done towards breaking the cycle of rural
poverty. If we will deal with each situation as it arises, before it becomes
complicated, we will not have to worry about precedents, nor shall they
bog us down. Responding quickly to each other, we will carry out our
responsibility without having to depend on specialists. South Sudanese
bishops in their pastoral letter *"Behold, I Make All Things New"*, affirmed
this attitude and spirit in encouraging everyone to move together for the
growth of the one nation:

> From past experience, we bishops have realised that the true spirit of unity has
> been waning; this has led to the weakening of our constructive capacity to gain
> our rights … [as] citizens of this nation. Personal interests, tribalism, greed,
> our passivity in the face of injustice, hunger and oppression have destroyed
> the fibre of our unity. This necessarily, brought us to the shocking realisation
> that all our rights, freedoms, and our identity have been snatched away from
> us. "It is now time for us to awaken from sleep" (*Rom* 13:11).[16]

One thing we will have to do, if we wish to change the present state of
affairs, is to constantly nurture an integrating outlook across generations,
across sexes, across religions, classes, tribal or ethnic groups, languages,
etc. We need to nurture this feeling in all our actions, big or small. Eventually it will become an integral part of us.

Externalisation of the problem appears to be a direct offshoot of a
fragmented identity. When there is fragmentation, one part is afraid of
the other parts. Because of fear, intermixing is avoided. This enhances
deprivation, prejudice and mutual distrust. Since the other is observed at
a distance, there is a lack of clarity about the other. So we quickly become
experts in passing the buck. Everyone blames everybody else. The many
ethnic groups in South Sudan have not been able to trust each other and
to see the good that lies in the other. Apparent friendship among some of
these groups is always nurtured by political favours and superficial flattery.

Instead, the problems between ethnic groups, parents and children,
teachers and students, workers and management, consumers and produc-
ers, have to be solved by coming together on the understanding that they
are part of the problem. The whole approach would then progressively
change: from fear, suspicion, wild allegations and violence to mutual
respect, understanding, intermixing and sharing.

---

[16] Sudan Catholic Bishops' Conference, *Letters to the Church of South Sudan,* Khartoum 2000, p
230, § 2.

South Sudan Can Reverse Its History of Violence

The answer is in our history and in ourselves, since it calls for both individual and collective responses. Beyond doubt, viewing and recalling South Sudan's history of tragedies, one may automatically feel dejected and dismayed, and conclude that the portrayal of the national and situational violence in our country makes achieving peace an impossible attempt. Maybe, also, a good number of well-intentioned people may feel helpless and think that a national level uprising for national reconstruction is not feasible in a sickening atmosphere vitiated by massive and continued violence. And then there are also those who wish for and love violence as a rod of power, accepting, as was claimed by Mao Zedung, that "power comes from the barrel of a gun."[17]

Military power has long been regarded as essential to the security of the State and military victory over the enemy, who may or may not have been the aggressor, has always been glorified. Gil Baillie's opinion of violence runs thus:

> There have been periods in history in which episodes of terrible violence occurred but for which the word violence was never used ... Violence is shrouded in justifying myths that lead to moral legitimacy, and these myths for the most part kept people from recognising the violence for what it was. The people who burnt witches at the stake never for one moment thought of their act as violence, rather they thought of it as an act of divinely mandated righteousness. The same can be said of most of the violence we humans have ever committed.[18]

This feeling may get further strengthened by a day to day unfolding of terrifying events, of shocking and shameful revelations of high-level killings, poverty, mistrust, hunger, bombardments of innocent people, etc. Here, the wise words of Jeannette Rankin can inspire us to rethink our attitude towards violence: "You can no more win a war than you can win an earthquake."[19]

It is not that we do not know some of the causes for the maladies affecting South Sudan. It is also not that we do not know that there are remedies to cure them. The solution cannot be another violent act, it has

---

[17] See the description of Mao Zedung's luxurious life in HARRISON SALISBURY, *The New Emperors: China in the Era of Mao and Deng"*, Little Brown, Boston 1992, especially part two: "The Secret Life of Zhangnanhai".

[18] Gil Bailie, winner of the 1996 Pax Christi Book, *Award for Violence Unveiled,* made this mark in an interview. See *Catholic Peace Voice,* quarterly publication of Pax Christi, USA, Fall 1996, p. 8.

[19] Warisstupid.com" website, http://www.hickorytech.net/waristupid/page2/ downloaded on 14/03/2004.

to be a peaceful one. Gandhi warned against revenge, because it means doing violence to ourselves:

> It is quite proper to resist and attack a system, but to resist and attack its author is tantamount to resisting and attacking oneself. For we are all tarred with the same brush, and are children of one and the same creator, and as such the divine powers within us are infinite. To slight a single divine being is to slight those divine powers, and thus to harm not only that being but with him the whole world.[20]

Unfortunately, what we lack are dedicated, well-informed, broad-minded and selfless leaders to lead and manage all South Sudanese into a remarkable revolution for peace building. South Sudan needs selfless leadership, and a people-based peaceful revolution without hero-worship is the need of the hour. Fear needs to be replaced by the courage of conviction. Our hope is in all people of good will in South Sudan and in those who have genuine interest in the progress of South Sudan. The command of the Lord Jesus Christ can unite the people's aspiration for peace, to ignore hate and enemies for a genuine purpose. "You have heard that it was said, 'you shall love your neighbour and hate your enemy.' But I say to you, love your enemies, and pray for those who persecute you" (Matthew 5:43-44). This commandment of love sets no boundaries; as such it makes it easier for all to work together for the interest of all.

Politics Must Be *of* the People and *for* the People

It is equally important to consider some of the key elements and organs needed for the construction of permanent peace in South Sudan. For peace to be genuine, it must include the government machinery or apparatus that has the goal of enhancing the benefits of permanent peace: a) governance b) economy c) security d) social development through justice and reconciliation.

Governance

South Sudan has a background of successive governments of Islamic-led leadership that were characterised by military dictatorship, a strong nationwide security presence and centralisation of power and wealth. Basic social services for many marginalised people were not a priority for such regimes.

---

[20] GANDHI, in RICHARD L. JOHNSON – ERIC LEDBETTER, *Peace and Change,* vol. 22, n. 1, January 1997 p. 34.

The government, by its nature, should have something of a special autonomy or democratic rule. This would make people feel that their safety and social welfare has been secured and improved. It would enhance educational opportunities for all South Sudanese and would provide for their fair and equal representation in all walks of life, especially in the public sector. In the words of Amartya Sen, "a good government guarantees the possibility of 'rethinking the idea of development and peace."[21]

This is how the government has to reinforce the efforts of officials at all levels to improve local capacity for improved government, including management, budgeting and administration. A government can be well sustained only when it has strong economic power.

Economy

The continuous civil war in South Sudan has deprived the country of systematic growth and stability. South Sudan's national economy is plagued by high levels of debt, both external and domestic. Problems are compounded by a dearth of foreign investors and an overall loss of investor confidence. The deterioration of capital stock impedes equipment modernisation, which, in turn, undermines economic performance and limits job opportunities. More than half of the population survives on less than $0.5 a day.

Of particular concern to South Sudan's immediate economic recovery are the less than strong national policies and legislation governing petroleum and mineral extraction. In addition, social tensions are exacerbated by the fact that local industries, including most retail businesses, are not well diffused. In South Sudan, there is a direct link between economic development and conflict prevention. Measures should be adopted to expand the stake of the local population in development of natural resources, so that resource exploitation may contribute to improving the living conditions of all South Sudanese. Sen views the economy as similar to every structure of human life and existence and, as such, it must be well taken care of, for the growth of the nation:

> Economics has had two rather different origins, both related to politics, but related in rather different ways, concerned respectively with "ethics" on one hand, and with what may be called "engineering" on the other hand (...) The "engineering" approach is characterised by being concerned with primarily logistic issues rather than with ultimate ends and such questions as what may foster "the good man" or "how one should live." The ends are taken as fairly

---

[21] SEN AMARTYA, *Resources, Values and Development,* Cambridge, 1997, p. 32.

straightforwardly given, and the object of the exercise is to find the appropriate means to serve.[22]

Furthermore, national and international corporations operating in South Sudan can help by adopting sustained and enhanced training and hiring programmes for South Sudanese, enabling South Sudanese to share in economic benefits through affirmative action in employment preferences. They could also expand special compensation and more effectively deliver social services. Innovative financing schemes are needed for small- and medium-sized businesses owned by the local population. Training and education programmes that would foster professional skills and improve the understanding of economic processes and opportunities are also greatly needed.

Security

Reformed, competent, accountable security services are essential for a democratically developing South Sudan. The army should be trained to carry out its national functions of protecting the country and preserving the citizens in peace. According to W.W. Rostow, a political economist, there are five successive historical stages through which the background societies must pass in order to become modern and peaceful:

> Traditional societies are mainly agricultural and characterised by low productivity. The second stage, the preconditions for take-off, is stimulated by intrusions from the more advanced societies. These normally take the form of technology transfers, leading to an expansion in trade and consequent economic growth. In addition it is assumed that a path in economic growth will lead to the political constitution of a national (independent) state of managing the economy. Thus peace prevails. During this period of take-off, growth becomes a permanent feature in the economy. This is the key stage in the process; achieved by an increase in the rate of capital investment ... Growth becomes automatic .... Development is thus a basically indigenous process that is growing from within. Better-trained, adequately paid, and more accountable security forces are essential to providing necessary law, order and security, while decreasing resentments that fuel violence.[23]

Social Development

The greatest impact of a just and non-discriminatory system would be to enforce equal distribution of wealth and revenues to all local authorities in the country. If funds and wealth were disbursed and local authorities

---

[22] Ibid., p. 34.
[23] Ibid., p. 3.

applied them in the service of social development, this would have a significant impact on the lives of South Sudanese people. Such a law and system would strengthen traditional social institutions, reaffirm traditional customary law, and create institutions to give voice to local people's aspirations and promote indigenous rights. This would lead to the creation of village consultative bodies and would provide for the resolution of land conflicts via traditional mediation mechanisms.

A vibrant civil society with trust between citizens and government organisations is needed to ensure that South Sudanese derive the maximum possible benefit from any law or system aiming to develop South Sudan. Civil society participation would also create confidence among the people of South Sudan and this law or system would result in measurable benefits to their quality of life. "Without a strong civil society, illegal activity will grow and corrupt officials will misappropriate the revenues."[24] Civil society can help law-enforcement organisations curtail illicit activities and prevent violence of all sorts.

Better schooling, health care and social development would reverse the trend of marginalisation. As a starting point for improving the education sector, a comprehensive assessment should be undertaken of infrastructure, accessibility, qualifications, teacher-student ratios, retention rates, curriculum and language of instruction. Discussions about improving education should involve teachers, families and other civil-society representatives. Primary health care and maternal and child health are priorities. Improved environmental protection is needed in urban areas and near development projects. During this long civil war in South Sudan, wild life heritage has been put at risk. For example, at certain points, some unruly soldiers were able to use grenade bombs to catch fish. By exploding grenades in rivers, they kill all living creatures in the rivers.

Traditional forms of mediation and conflict prevention are essential to the maintenance of social order and for the realisation of more harmonious inter-ethnic, inter-politcal and interfaith relations.

By working with international donors and multinational corporations, civil society groups can use their access to communities across the states to improve humanitarian conditions. Community leaders, institutions, Church groups, and mosques, whose respect is unparalleled at the grassroots level, are essential service providers and are very useful for community organising.[25]

---

[24] Cf. DAVID RODEN, *After Three Years. The Present State of the South Sudan,* 1975, p. 35.

[25] Excerpts from World Summit on Sustainable Development, Johannesburg August 26th – September 4th 2002 (http://www.un.or/esa/sustdev/ agreed.htm), downloaded 04.04.2003.

Yes, it is possible to overcome violence and all the problems that have emerged as a result. Our model of confronting these things must be like that of Jesus, crucified and risen, "who destroyed death and brought life and immortality to light through the gospel" (2 Timothy 1:10). Peace can prevail when justice and reconciliation are at work.

Justice and Reconciliation Are Instruments

'Justice' refers to the quality of being just and fair, to the principle of moral rightness, equity, conformity to moral rightness in action or attitude. It is the upholding of what is just, it is fair treatment and due reward in accordance with honour, standards, or law, it is conformity to truth or sound reason. There will be no way forward for South Sudan unless the country embarks on the implementation of justice, healing and reconciliation programmes at all levels, right up to the national level. In order to get the point right, we must determine what kind of reconciliation we are talking about, and what reconciliation is most appropriate for South Sudanese people. This will help avoid wrong connotations. The word 'reconciliation' can be used in many different ways: reconciliation of financial bills, reconciliation of administrative disputes, reconciliation of apparently contradictory facts, reconciliation of broken families and also sacramental reconciliation of sinners. Here the word is being used to refer to the social recovery of a society following decades of violence.

When we look more closely at reconciliation, we can see a lot of differences in the ways that it is being perceived and used by people who are all aiming at one thing only: PEACE. True reconciliation cannot succeed when the means of looking for it are too rushed. On many occasions, this is what people who cause violence themselves are doing, perhaps to cover their guilty consciences and to buy time. Another trick is when an atmosphere of peace is being created by appeasing those who have been victimised, making them forget the past suffering while the oppressors continue in their leadership with little or no attention being paid to the victims. These are not reconciliations, since the victim of violence and his or her suffering is being forgotten, and the causes of the suffering are never uncovered or confronted again. In the words of Robert Schreiter the causes of violence should be searched for, for a proper diagnosis to be applied:

If the causes of suffering are not addressed, suffering is likely to continue; the wheel of violence keeps turning, and more and more people get crushed.[26]

The problem, the challenge as such, to be sorted out is: Who is going to develop and uphold the machinery of a justice and reconciliation process in South Sudan after the war, (presuming that the war will, at some stage, come to an end)? Transitional justice includes strategies for prosecuting perpetrators, uncovering the truth regarding human rights violations, reforming abusive institutions, providing reparations to victims and promoting reconciliation. The greatest challenge of the immediate post-war period will lie in the setting up of a generally acceptable process of justice and reconciliation. During this transitional period, the truth with regard to human rights violations will have to be established and the perpetrators dealt with accordingly. Recompense will have to be made to the victims of injustice, abusive institutions will have to be reformed and ways and means of promoting reconciliation will have to be put in place. A successful strategy balances retrospective endeavours, which may seek to document and acknowledge human rights abuses and pursue accountability for past crimes, with prospective initiatives aiming at building institutions that uphold the rule of law and promote genuine reconciliation after violence. This is the kind of procedure that is needed in order to avoid a quick rebirth of another civil war. But there is also another way to solve problems such as ours, and that is by following in the footsteps of Jesus Christ, who intimately changed the culture of violence, as Daniel Berrigan wrote:

In a fallen world, we will probably always have some forms of violence. But the question is what part can Christians play in such a situation? To say that the world is fallen and sinful is not to say all that needs to be said. We still have the Sermon on the Mount and the example of Jesus Christ.[27]

There is also a strong need for an anti-violence movement to be developed in South Sudan, and the leaders of all religious, civic and tribal groups, as well as academics and members of the police force, must be encouraged to participate fully in this campaign. Peaceful stratagems must be set in place to provide alternatives to violence in the settlement

---

[26] Notes from Robert Schreiter, who gave presentations on _Violence, Peacemaking and Reconciliation: Challenges for Religious Communities_ during a conference organised by the Commission for Justice, Peace and Integrity held at the Generalate of the Brothers of the Christian Schools, November 28-29th 2003, Rome.

[27] DANIEL BERRIGAN, "Who Dies First: the Gunman or the Victim?" in _The Center Magazine_, vol. 19, May-June 1986, p. 22.

of grievances and foreign powers must be strongly discouraged from the sale of armaments into this strife-torn country.

Peace, healing and justice will, in effect, only come to prevail when we have learned to act in accordance with the teachings of Jesus Christ, encapsulated in the Sermon on the Mount. It is only by showing a loving and compassionate understanding of the grievances of others that we will be able to defuse their feelings of aggression towards us. One of the tasks of the anti-violence movement will be to hold several peace seminars, peace congresses and peace conferences. This gradually will create a culture of peace among South Sudanese war victims.

A process for addressing human rights abuses, while taking into account South Sudan's history of violence, is essential to bringing conflicts to an end. The oppression and distrust felt by many should be addressed. Lack of accountability fosters a vicious cycle of further human rights violations and increased radicalism on the part of the marginalised South Sudanese.

In their Message on the obligation of human rights, the Association of Member Episcopal Conferences in Eastern Africa (AMECEA) bishops said:

> No member of the human family can claim authority before God to deny human rights and social justice to another member of that human family on the grounds of race, colour, tribe, religion, political views or condition of life in any country .... We condemn all unjust laws, harmful political pressures and acts of oppression from any civil power.[28]

Better pay for local officials would help minimise corruption. Dispute resolution mechanisms should draw on people's traditions and should include substantial community dialogue involving all people, elders, women and the youth, as well as inter-ethnical traditional peace rituals and reconciliatory atonement, etc. Interfaith and women's movements are also pivotal partners in creating a dialogue to address South Sudan's long history of violence and to promote improved inter-group relations.

Common experience indicates that 'truth and reconciliation' initiatives are effective only if all parties, but particularly those who have suffered human rights abuses, feel confident that the past will be investigated in an open and independent manner. Efforts to pursue truth and reconciliation will fail if sons and daughters of South Sudan feel that the emphasis placed on national unity is impeding an honest examination of the past. Conversely, the government has much to gain if these individuals feel that

---

[28] Pontifical Council for Justice and Peace, *The Challenge of Justice and Peace, The Response of the Church in Africa*, Libreria Editrice Vaticana (ed. B. Murano), Vatican City 1998, pp. 71-72.

their long and dreadful suffering has been properly acknowledged and if appropriate remedial measures are adopted. To be effective, the truth and the reconciliation process must not be regarded as a manipulated political process, a substitute for accountability, or a means to grant amnesty for violations of human rights.

More emphasis must be put on religious, ethnic-based and tribal organisations, to continue their dialogue on peaceful resolution of disputes. Donor resources must be used to institutionalise the dialogue through the strengthening of a permanent governing body.

Reconciliation Means Being Responsible: Moral Evaluation

When we speak of reconciliation, it means that we are addressing the behaviour and activities of a human person. His activities may be pleasing to him and others or may be depriving the other members of the community of their God-given rights. A true human action always occurs in specific contexts and has effects that go beyond the individual person. Thus the barrier between human action and social action becomes fuzzy, and the two are united by the reality of responsibility. This being the case, an accusing finger runs from leaders to leaders that have been the cause of South Sudan's state of violence and lack of peace. It is because of the bad impact of man's acts upon his neighbour that he would need to assume responsibility for his actions and move to normalise his relations with his neighbour – hence reconciliation.

Experiences have plenty of examples for us to understand what it means to be responsible. This sense of responsibility is associated with what one does or what one is expected to do. This is true for community leaders, lawyers, judges, parents, administrators and others who are concerned with issues of responsibility: they know, or think they know, what the conditions of responsibility are. Their questions are questions of application: does this or that particular person meet this or that particular condition? Is this person mature enough, or informed enough … was he acting under the influence of a mind-impairing drug? It is assumed, in these contexts, that normal, fully developed adult human beings are responsible beings.[29]

To be able to speak or seek reconciliation, one is thought to be able to understand or admit his social actions. He should have the capacity to

---

[29] Cf. S. REHRAUER, *Responsibility and the Human Person: Its Nature and Attribution in Moral Theology and Contribution of Psychological Theories of Attribution,* Doctoral Dissertation: Comillas Pontificial University, Madrid, Spain 1996, p. 19.

identify the impact that his actions may have upon his fellow human be-ings. If one fails to feel responsible, he cannot be able to move towards reconciliation. The portrait of South Sudan's history of violence, as is shown in the previous chapters, establishes a strong sense of collective condemnation of people believed to have caused the misery of our people. Yes, of course there exists a collective responsibility for group activity, because human personhood is intimately interpersonal and truly human action is a social reality. A truly human action is fundamentally social. Human action is meaningful and meaning is an interpersonal and shared reality. We are all, at one and the same time, both responsible for others and for the responsibility of others.

A common criticism levelled against the use of the concept of collective responsibility is that it attempts to hold individuals morally responsible for actions which they themselves have not performed, and that this violates the principle of Justice. Persons can only be held responsible for what they have done, not for what others have done.

Since responsibility is reciprocal, a role-bearing individual is responsi-ble to his social groups for the fulfilment of his interpersonal task, but his social group also has a responsibility to him. Furthermore, responsibility is directly tied to power (capacity), and the exercise and apportionment of power is ultimately linked to one's membership in a social group.[30]

But the point is: can the descendents of, for example, slave traders still be held responsible for what took place many centuries ago? At that time, slavery was considered to be morally acceptable and was widely practised. In those times and places, people who owned slaves were not considered immoral persons. It was only with the passage of time and the changes in the structure and content of moral understanding that human slavery developed into a human evil and became considered as immoral, the reprobate behaviour that it truly is. But Africans felt immediately that slavery was an evil against them. As such, many did fight back. No Af-rican thought it to be morally good to sell another human being as slave. Africans had expected humanity to apologise, if not to offer compensation, but such expectations were in vain.

Reconciliation is effective only when we can know the depth of the offence. This is the fundamental problem of collective responsibility. Who can answer for everyone, for what we all do, and for what we all believe to be morally right, even when it causes great suffering to others? Who, for example, was or is responsible for the institutionalised practice of

---

[30]   B. HÄRING, *Sin in the Secular Age,* Edizioni Paoline 1975, p. 19.

slavery? Slavery and other social evils that have been committed in the past are the responsibility of people who died in the past.

Reconciliation is only talked about and sought after the mistake or damage has already been caused. An offence committed in the past is always forgiven in the present. Reconciliation, in other words, is the restoration or replacement of past evil with present good. Reconciliation comes to rebuild whatever has been destroyed.

The question of historical responsibility arises most clearly when conditions of widespread social evil have become institutionalised. First of all, because of the reality of human solidarity and the unity of human history, all people can, in a certain sense, be considered morally responsible for the events of human history. Rather than culpability for what was done by others in the past, it is more a metaphysical recognition of the demand to respond to what pertains to our historical present.[31] In terms of moral culpability, as in the example of slavery and massacre, each is considered to be morally responsible for the measure in which he freely and deliberately practises or refuses to practise that evil, or on the basis of how he follows or fails to follow the moral law. However, since the knowledge of good and evil is socially delineated, taught, communicated, and reinforced by means of punishment and reward according to the existing norms of a given society, what happens to freedom and knowledge when these very norms and the processes of their socialisation become corrupt and when they prescribe evil as being good?[32]

People who do some injustice against their own people must know that it is quite necessary to change their life for the good of all. More precisely, one bears an obligation to contribute to, and purify, the moral understanding of one's social world. Personal responsibility becomes responsibility for the world, because the person and the world are inseparable. As human persons, our actions are creative. They have effects upon the world, upon the others, and upon our own selves. By our actions we actualise or negate transcendent value, alter or reaffirm the past, and direct the future in the context of a present moment. If basic responsibility is our capacity to respond, and moral responsibility is our capacity to respond creatively and consciously, and if every response has impacts upon the configuration of both our individual and social moral character, then we can highlight various areas for which we are responsible.

---

[31]　Cf. S. REHRAUER, *La responsibilità: Sfida e esigenza morale nel mondo contemporaneo*, Class Notes. Accademia Alfonsiana, Rome 2004.
[32]　Cf. ibid.

Catholic liturgical celebrations start with reconciliation gestures, where each and every participant declares himself or herself sorry and responsible for his or her mistakes. The traditional Catholic liturgical practice makes use of a very concise statement of moral responsibility:

> I confess to Almighty God, and to you, my brothers and sisters, that I have sinned, through my own fault, in my thoughts and in my words, in what I have done, and in what I have failed to do; and I ask blessed Mary ever virgin, and all the Angels and Saints, and you my brothers and sisters, to pray for me to the Lord our God.

Every one learns, at least individually, the values that lie in knowing and doing good. Parents always distinguish before their children all those values that are necessary for healthy growth. The prescription to do what is good and avoid what is evil arises from the call of every human person to convert himself into the image of God in the world. Since God is goodness itself, it is fundamental that the primary way in which a human being responds to that call is by means of personal goodness. Implicit in this principle is a derivative principle based on human nature: become good by doing what is good. Basically, here is where a human being controls the ground on which he freely chooses to reconcile with his fellow human being. Reconciliation can only be born when both the victim and perpetrator assume their own responsibility to move towards a new reality, which their faiths can dictate upon them.[33]

Speaking and seeking reconciliation for the sake of peace for the wronged and the oppressor is well understood within the demands of faith. Reconciliation is very much attached to the goodness of God, who is the Good himself. Actually, implementation of these capacities is fortified within the context of faith, because the ability to do these things is given within the context of salvation. It is the union with Christ that makes this integrity possible, and this union takes place within the community, which is his Church, the reconciled family. Within this social context of the Christian community, through reconciliation the human persons become united. One is able to respond "yes" to the call of being because, as a member of the faith community, one is united with the very "yes" itself, that is, the Word of God. From this unity derives the *raison d'être* of the Church which is to place human persons into contact with Christ, and, through Christ, with God.[34] The more intimately a human person is in contact with

---

[33] B. Haring, *Sin in the Secular Age*, p. 111.
[34] Cf. S. Rehrauer, *Responsibility and the Human Person*, op. cit., pp. 41-43.

God, the more united his individual being to the very source of all being, the more clearly he will be able to recognise the good, the more capable he will be of choosing the good, and the more prone he will be to act in a way which realises goodness. In this sense, it makes all the sense in the world to say that one does good because one is good, and to assume that one who consistently does evil has chosen to become evil. In either case, every action and every response to action has a moral significance. The spirit of reconciliation in human society becomes easier to experience because men have God as reason for their being.

Why are we as Christians morally responsible for reconciliation? Why should the Christian be the prototypical example of *The Reconciliator,* interpreting the events of people and the world according to a vision of faith and responding in a fitting manner? Because it is moral responsibility that makes human living truly possible.

Reconciliation is realised through the proper end of justice and peace. This creates in every human person the desire to reach one another for the purpose of peace. Why are we as Christians answerable to anyone? Because the very nature of our existence as a redeemed and sanctified community of human beings demands it. We are, as the presence of Christ in the world, both a source and a response to the existential tension of human reality. We offer a challenge, at times a threat, to the established way of seeing and responding to what is going on, and we offer a particular way of responding. God has chosen us to share in his creative activity. We are co-creators of reality with him, and it is only when we participate properly in this process of communication with him that we can even be said to be persons. Unless we are able to say with full conviction that alone I am not human, in isolation from others I am not a full human person (the African philosophy says: I am because we are), we will never be able to become fully what we truly are. The concept and activity of Christian moral responsibility makes this affirmation possible. If I am accountable to someone for who and what I am and do, for what I create and destroy; if I cannot even become truly myself without the other who demands of me a response; then I can never forget that it is essential to my nature that I form relationships with others, and with the absolute Other.[35]

The responsibility of the Church is to be a community of being goodness, of reconciliation and peace building, and those who, as members, belong to this community have a wide variety of calls to which they must respond.

---

[35]   Cf. ibid., p. 51.

They have, if you will, a greater role of responsibility than others, because they have been given a greater capacity to respond. Part of the responsibility they have will be to increase their capacity to respond, and this is the purpose of the sacramental life of the community which, if properly responded to, creates a link between moral action and personal being. Another aspect of their responsibility is to be leaven for the world, converting it by means of their own positive response to the call of being inserted in the kingdom of God. Their readiness to forgive their oppressors and their involvement in restoring a violent broken world into a peaceful society for humans to live in is what makes them real children of the God of peace. For a Christian, the morality of responsibility is seen not so much in terms of doing the right thing, but in terms of being goodness itself, a goodness that is expressed in doing the right things, which is supported within a faith context, and which is actualised in a social environment of meaning that is interpersonal and relational.[36] This goodness derives from union with Goodness itself. True responsibility in this sense is one with the reality of salvation. To be truly Christian is to be causally responsible for bringing about what is good. To be truly Christian is to be morally responsible for one's good actions. To be truly Christian is to be good. To be good in our context is to be a promoter of reconciliation and peace in the violent world.

Summary

The Greek philosopher Socrates once said that the end is in the beginning. Therefore, South Sudan's problems surely will come to end. It will depend on the patriotic spirit of each South Sudanese to see to it that their country is rebuilt into a peaceful nation for all.

There are ways and means to prevent South Sudan from entering into a new escalation of violence, if only the present conflict can be stopped by some inspired people. These inspired people must be on fire with the love of their nation, and must be clever at accommodating all people's differences to the benefit of the common good. In the words of Gil Bailie, people must live the love of God; this will prevent them from giving in to more violence:

> Jesus' ethic is clear: to suffer violence rather than inflict it. As Christians, we are called to imitate him. We will fail, but when we do, let's not return home from our failure to ticker-tape parades. Let's fall on our knees and pray for

---

[36] Cf. ibid., p. 52.

God's forgiveness. If the question is: is there any violence for which I would not need to repent after having committed it? The answer is no.[37]

This process cannot be forced or manipulated; it must be born from a consciousness and innate vision of one's country and human destiny.

Education and genuine formation of the citizen, old and young, stand the best chance of guiding a nation corrupted by a long history of violence. This education or formation must include essential elements of national interest and pride, which will eventually motivate the already downtrodden people to a vital outlook and commitment.

A sense of hope and new beginning can easily be reinforced, if the system involved is worthy of trust. As such, much attention must be paid to this delicate mission.

Peace can be imposed by the international community, but both international bodies and local people must feel responsible for the protection and guidance of that peace. They need to be ready to undertake immediate tasks if alterations may seem necessary. The implementation of justice and reconciliation after conflict is always an ideal but much care is needed to guarantee a positive result for the devastated nation.

The notion of responsibility in actualising the project of reconciliation is very much linked to the make-up of the human person. The human person is the image of God in the world, transcendent freedom and subjectivity actualising itself through human action within a temporal world of social and contextual meaning. Human action, in turn, is that activity which is not in keeping with the nature of personhood. Hence, human action is adaptive and purposeful by nature, and is informed by and comprised of two structural directions: the individual and the cultural. True human action always occurs in contexts and has effects that go beyond the individual person.

This way of looking at the human person as the image of God must take into account and integrate the realities of the person: transcendence, individuality and sociality. "Human nature has to be understood completely, with all its constitutive elements ... rationality, freedom, social character, relations of interdependence, man as planner, man as self-manipulating and self-transcending being."[38]

This comprehension of human nature reveals that man has to admit his shortcomings, sins, hate, and desire for revenge to move to something

[37] Gil Bailey, Interview by the Catholic Peace Voice, op. cit., p. 9.
[38] Cf. S. REHRAUER, *I a responsabilità. Sfida e esigenza,* op. cit.,

worthy. Reconciliation, as a value, is most needed by a wounded society, and people can uphold it, since reconciliation is goodness itself.

Moral responsibility is possible and necessary for human society. In the whole of Creation, it is human beings alone that want to be happy and live in peace; as such, they can transcend the evil of their society and create a society of peace.

Our Christian moral understanding of the value and need for reconciliation benefits from certain fundamental moral insights of Jesus: for example, "you can tell a tree by its fruits" (Mt 7:17 f.), and that "wicked designs come from the deep recesses of the heart... (Mt 15:19); all these evils come from within and render a man impure. There is an intimate link between the action a person performs and the person who performs the action. Before the choice and the performance of an act, which unleashes goodness or evil, there must already be something in the person that makes him capable of the choice to do so. On the other hand we have the example of Jesus' sensibility, his capacity to see beyond the specific actions of an individual and interpret them within the wider context and pattern of the temporal flow of one's life: "I tell you, that is why her many sins are forgiven her ... because of her great love" (Lk 7:47). Evil persons perform acts of evil, but good persons often also do. Within the most public of sinners – the Samaritan – there resides core goodness, while judges and priests are at times uncaring in the name of value and duty.[39]

Jesus also speaks of the intimate link between the individual person and other persons: "As often as you did it for one of my least brothers, you did it for me" (Mt 25:40), and of how the actions of one person, or of a small group, have effects upon all: "... you will come to the same end unless you reform" (Lk 13:5).

We can only come to a genuine reconciliation when we are able to believe in the power of responsibility. South Sudanese are the only builders and constructors of South Sudan. We do that because we are responsible. Only by South Sudanese themselves can the difficult history of South Sudan and the lack of peace be transformed into real reconciliation. But to be reconciled, one must first be responsible.

I bring this chapter to a close with the prayer and intention for Africa of His Holiness John Paul II, in his traditional Message for the World Day of Peace, 2005:

---

[39] Cf. ibid.

May the peoples of Africa become the protagonists of their own future and their own cultural, civil, social and economic development! May Africa cease to be a mere recipient of aid, and become a responsible agent of convinced and productive sharing! Achieving this goal calls for a new political culture.

During this year dedicated to the *Eucharist*, may the sons and daughters of the Church find in the *supreme sacrament of love* the wellspring of all communion: communion with Jesus the Redeemer and, in him, with every human being.[40]

Questions for Reflection

1. The long and desperate series of conflicts in South Sudan has had an impact on every South Sudanese. Can it be said that "to bring peace" is the responsibility of every South Sudanese? And how?

2. What moral responsibility is appropriate for each South Sudanese, in order to reach permanent peace?

3. Since South Sudanese follow several different religious beliefs, they probably have various concepts of reconciliation, peace, goodness and human rights notion. What do you think is a common thread for everyone to seek peace through reconciliation?

4. What benefit does a person receive when he is in command of his responsibility?

5. Christian moral responsibility is built on the truth that every human person is made in the image of God, who is the source of all that is good. Can this concept be valid in working for peace?

6. The process of peacebuilding through reconciliation is time-consuming. How can the notion 'responsibility for reconciliation' become more progressive?

7. Do you think that you have a responsibility to contribute to achieving peace in South Sudan?

8. What do you think are some existing positive elements and visible signs to obtaining peace and reconciliaiton?

---

[40] JOHN PAUL II, *World Peace Day, 2005*, pp. 13-16.

CHAPTER THREE

Negotiation in a Time of Crisis

I have spent time in the previous chapters laying bare the ugliness of war, unjust structures, violence and instability whose impact has shattered the entire fabric of South Sudan. To unpack such huge devastation, we must humbly employ dialogue, discussion and negotiations, leaving no stone unturned. The complexity of the problems in South Sudan can only be resolved through a well intentioned and mutually open dialogue. Ultimately, negotiations quite often happen in the context of established relationships, or they take place within established social structures, such as the legal system or corporate settings.

Those who take on the delicate role of negotiators ought to encounter one another within relationships and structures that are generally peaceful and widely accepted as legitimate, enabling them to work within a relatively stable sense of reality. In such an event, relationships and interactions need to be governed by mutually understood norms and rules. These norms and rules have to be enforced through voluntarily accepted cultural understandings about how things ought to be done, or through formal rules of behaviour or contractual obligations, or some combination of the two. This means that, in stable settings, the parties can focus on their encounter with one another rather than on managing changes in their surroundings that might affect their relationship.

What is meant by a "stable setting"? You have to provide mechanisms that support the negotiation process, including:

- Fostering a mutually accepted rule of behaviour;
- Developing together shared norms of fairness;
- There must be a relative certainty that the negotiators have a shared future; and
- Importantly, institutions (formal or informal) that can enforce negotiated agreements must be in place for proper implementation of negotiated agreements.

For us in South Sudan, it is a difficult, and sometimes embarrassing situation, to ask questions such as: How do we negotiate when life gets messy? How does an unstable environment alter the process of negotiation? How do we negotiate with one another when the institutions and structures that support negotiation are broken or missing? How do we negotiate with one another when we don't share common understandings about how we should negotiate? These and other questions can come up especially when we evaluate the many months that have been spent negotiating for a peaceful settlement to South Sudan's conflict.

Experiences show that, during times of social change, such as that change that our nation is now going through, those mechanisms that support negotiation are unclear, fragile, or completely missing. The parties negotiate in contexts in which there are likely to be:

- Uncertain or disputed rules of behaviour;
- Competing norms of fairness;
- Uncertainty that they have a shared future; and
- Broken, non-existent, or controversial institutions or mechanisms for enforcing negotiated agreements.

Talking about Negotiation Is Necessary!

Many people have complained about unnecessary delays in the South Sudanese peace talks. They have protested against the seemingly lack of political will in handling the South Sudan peace talks. The Intergovernmental Authority on Development (IGAD) and all the various envoys and stakeholders involved in the South Sudanese peace initiative have encountered huge obstacles. There have been frustrations over who should be involved in the process, and there have been times when some issues have been finally agreed upon, only to have new parties and new issues emerge to upset the agreement. This chapter will bring more light to these challenges. Negotiated peace settlements do not achieve peace in and of themselves, but rather they are a paved road map that, through reconciliation, may lead to permanent peace.

The approach here is mainly to expose one major area as an example of how to address negotiation phenomena. We will look firstly at how to deal with a complicated environmental issue, that is, how to negotiate during a turbulent situation. For me, it is not a recipe for negotiation; rather this is an invitation to participate in creative experimentation, rather than just assuming that difficult situations make negotiations impossible.

In our church language we always say that time heals. It is a principle of negotiations to have a peaceful environment for discussion. In stable settings, negotiators may choose to focus on short-term tactics: What moves will help me win this negotiation? Or they may choose a mix of tactics and strategies that focuses on managing relationships and problems over a longer time frame: How can I maximise my chances of winning this round while keeping the play (the broader relationship between the negotiators, which is something very crucial in peace negotiations) going so that I might win other rounds?

In an unstable setting, negotiators who try to focus only on the tactical level run the risk of losing even if they win. They may ultimately lose if the instability in their context makes implementing their agreement difficult or impossible. Sometimes changes in context turn what looks like victory into defeat. In an unstable setting, the negotiators who understand and respond effectively to the conflicts in their turbulent surroundings can negotiate their own problems more effectively and help bring stability to the larger system. To do this, they must think strategically about more than their relationship with the other negotiators at the table. They need to consider the way their negotiation game is embedded in, influenced by, and capable of altering the infinite game of the social relationships that make up the context in which they live and work.

Reasons for My Input

In February 2014, the Catholic Bishops of South Sudan, in their Metropolitan First Assembly of the year, selected me to participate in the IGAD-led South Sudan Mediation Process, as part of the Faith-Based Organisation set up under the South Sudan Council of Churches and the South Sudan Islamic Council. This assignment resonated with my desire to work for peace in my country, a job I have done for many years as Goodwill Ambassador. When I finally joined the teams of the Big 8 stakeholders, namely:

1. Government,

2. SPLM/SPLA in Opposition,

3. Former SPLM Leaders and Detainees,

4. Political Parties,

5. Civil Society Organisations,

6. Faith-Based Organisations,

7. Imminent personalities, and

8. The negotiators and their envoys.

After nearly eight months in this group, I find myself in the company of two different groups of people concerned with issues of conflict resolution or transformation for the Republic of South Sudan. One group, the negotiation scholars and professional negotiators, is inclined to think of negotiation as a finite game, even if that game is set inside an infinite game of human relationships. Many of them describe negotiation as if it always occurs in stable settings, with clear rules and boundaries and obvious winners and losers.

The second group, the peace activists and peace-builders, is inclined to view negotiation with deep suspicion. Many of them see the world as an uneven playing field on which powerful parties oppress weaker parties. Since weaker parties will inevitably lose the finite game of negotiation, it is better for them not to play the game at all. Peace will be created by focusing energy on changing the playing field and the rules of play, not by negotiating specific issues or problems with powerful oppressors.

Again and again, I have come to the conclusion that these two groups are both wrong in their approach. Those who treat negotiation as a finite game in a stable context minimise the full complexity of the conflicts that brought the parties to the negotiation table. They may negotiate agreements that put a small band-aid on deep-rooted and intractable conflicts, thereby creating greater social turmoil. The peace they win in these situations is fleeting at best. Then there are those who think that negotiation is always 'selling out' to the powerful parties. They focus on the sources of deep-rooted conflicts, but they overlook the option of negotiating strategically to transform conflict and change unjust social systems. Both groups would benefit from thinking about how to negotiate strategically in unstable settings.

Let me explain further what is meant by negotiating strategically in an unstable context. It, essentially, involves:

Focusing both on the immediate problems and the long-term relationships between the parties;

Managing both the context of turmoil and the interactions at the negotiation table;

- Working to bolster, create and sustain the social structure and the political will that supports the negotiation process, as well as the agreement reached by the negotiators.

Thinking of the Bigger Picture

It is paramount for peace negotiations to bear in mind the main priority: the human person in South Sudan and his or her dignity. Hence, to successfully negotiate problems in the absence of structures that organise and support the negotiation, negotiators must also manage activities that are normally handled in quiet, routine manners by established institutions. Consequently, they must depend on the goodwill and the support of other parties not at the table (particularly the grassroots people and their structures) to implement and sustain their agreement. No matter how fair and just an agreement is, others will not support it if the negotiators at the table do not consult with those who do not have a seat at the table.

As a matter of fact, extra care must be taken to ensure that primary negotiations involve those most relevant to the resolution of the issue. Sometimes, in such processes, we are shocked to find shadow negotiations taking place, involving parties that have a stake in the conflict but who have deliberately decided not to participate in the negotiation process.

In the final analysis, such institutions, bodies and organisations are often key players when it comes to implementing an agreement, but negotiators representing these parties are frequently only able to speak for one small portion of the organisation. Consequently, the internal negotiations within those organisations are extremely important when it comes to implementing and sustaining an agreement.

Surrounding the organised stakeholder groups is the general public of unorganised individuals who can be mobilised to either support or challenge a negotiated agreement. In good faith, and with God-given wisdom, if negotiators can pay attention to the needs of the general public, and plan ahead to present their agreement to the public and educate them about it, then such moves may save the agreed accord. It's important, however, that education and public consultation starts early on in the peace process, even before formal negotiations convene, and they must continue after an agreement is reached. This strategy will safeguard the public's interests and ensure a public buy-in to the process, eventually minimising the chances that groups will form to oppose the results of their negotiation.

Negotiations in Negotiated Environments

Peace negotiation involves parties who have a conflict or dispute discussing ways to find a nonviolent solution to their problem. Other times, negotiation may be done competitively: each party tries to maximise their own gains and minimise their own losses. Preferably, negotiation may be done cooperatively: the parties try to figure out how each party can get the most satisfactory solution to their problem. In most cases, parties move between competitive and cooperative approaches, depending on the issue, the nature of their relationship and a host of other factors.

South Sudan has a short institutional memory of what negotiation and its dimensions mean at the end of the day. In this regard, a hallmark of much negotiation literature is the idea that negotiators should present their positions (their stated objectives or goals), as well as what motivates their interests (what they really want) and what their needs are (what they actually need in order to survive).

When the ground-work has been done well, and willingness to negotiate has been generated, then we can say that one or more of the following situations have been reached:

- The participants in the process recognise their relationship with one another, but at least two parties (environmentalists and breeders) are also tied to other organisations that view this level of cooperation with suspicion;

- These parties accept that negotiation is the proper way to handle differences over the limited issues and problems they have identified, but they do not assume that negotiation is the only way they will manage their conflicts. They might at other times, or for other reasons, resort to litigation or other less cooperative activities;

- They acknowledge each other as legitimate negotiators for these issues, but much about the issues remains unclear;

- They will need to develop norms and expectations about negotiation since this is a new process for them;

- The parties probably do not recognise the legitimacy of the same potential arbiters ("referees" or "judges").

The drama or game could end well and peace could be achieved, or the game may terminate and the situation may deteriorate into more violence. This can happen when the negotiators or stakeholders reach an impasse in their negotiation. Therefore, failure in negotiation is likely to result in resumed hostility and confrontational tactics. For example, if the government or one of the principal negotiators to the conflict passes new legislation, perhaps at the behest of the environmentalist or breeders advocacy groups who are not participating in the negotiation, how will this affect the issues on the table and the relationships among the negotiators? Or if another environmental group sues the hosting agencies during the negotiation process, how will the parties respond?

Negotiating in this manner potentially threatens the participants' identities. We can readily see that relationships are fragile and the issues to be negotiated are complex. The turbulence surrounding the negotiations will also manifest itself in the negotiations themselves. It must be kept in mind that negotiation is never the only option for addressing conflicts. Therefore, parties considering negotiation need to ask:

- Is negotiation the best option for addressing our issues and problems? What are the alternatives to negotiation?
- If negotiation is the best option, to whom should we entrust with the delicate work of moderating the negotiation?

Parties should assess their best alternative to a negotiated agreement both before entering into negotiations and repeatedly during the negotiation process, since parties usually have the option to leave the negotiation if they so desire.

Finally, after a lot of substantial ground-work, if the parties decide to negotiate, then they need to be clear about the scope and limitations of negotiation, particularly in a context of change and instability. They need to identify:

- What problems or issues they will negotiate, and list these problems or issues in order of priority;
- What problems or issues they will address using other methods of conflict resolution;
- What other groups or parties need to be included in the negotiation process, and what groups or parties will be necessary for implementing the outcomes the negotiation; and
- How will the negotiation fit into other processes for managing specific problems or issues, how it will effect broader relationships, and what impact changing contexts may have on the negotiation.

Any instability in this process due to the negotiators may not be because of the fragile system within which they are negotiating, but may be because the negotiators themselves need to renegotiate their personal relationships and identities while working through the legal framework of peace negotiation.

Assuming that the parties to the conflict opt for negotiation, they first need to make some important strategic decisions. Do they want to negotiate face-to-face or through their intermediaries? Negotiating face-to-face allows space to address the problem of redefining personal relationships, thereby increasing control over the central source of turbulence. Face-to-face negotiation minimises the risk of miscommunication. It can also prevent the problem of the intermediaries focusing only on a small scope of the whole picture or on the legal issues of rights and responsibilities without taking into account the big picture of the whole nation. If they choose to use a mediator, they need to decide what kind of mediator they should employ. Attention must be paid to who is appointed mediator, as he or she may, at times, be less focused on reaching long-term solutions or preserving relationships than the parties themselves may be.

Negotiation requires a delicate balance between caution and hope. The parties need to know that what they are doing will not impose significant changes in the positions they, and other parties not at the table, hold. At the same time, they need to have some hope that lessons learned through this negotiation and the resulting experimental project might yield positive outcomes for what has been an intractable conflict. Ensuring that the parties are in fact committed to trying something radically new is also important, and this will need attention throughout the negotiation because pressures from other parties will affect the negotiators' calculation of risk and their ongoing commitment to the process.

The act of balancing caution and hope is complicated by identity issues. The participants may be prepared to identify with a radical centre, but few of them are ready to sever all of their ties with other groups. They will need those other groups if these negotiations fail, and they will need those groups to address the larger conflict.

Finally, the parties' positions are more likely to succeed in creating and sustaining a negotiation process if they coordinate the negotiation with other processes for addressing the broader conflict. Dialogue processes that involve other stakeholders may need to take place alongside negotiations. The parties may agree to negotiate one problem but reserve the right to sue one another over other problems. These limitations should be made as clear as possible when negotiations commence in order to avoid hard feelings and resentment later.

Managing Negotiations by Proxy

In many circumstances, when violence or conflicts have taken place, and continue to take place, seeking solutions from different sources are initiatives of good will. The parties in conflict always task their most trusted individuals with assisting in the peace negotiations. In such unstable contexts, the negotiators' decisions can have far-reaching effects, resulting in other people taking a keen interest in their work. Strategic negotiators learn how to make this outside interest work for the long-term benefit of the negotiated agreement. Rather than seeing "interested outsiders" as a nuisance, good strategic negotiators work with those outsiders to create a constituency that supports the agreement. This constituency is a necessary supplement to, or replacement of, the institutions that are supposed to enact and enforce negotiated agreements in stable settings.

It is helpful to think of strategic negotiation in an unstable environment as improvisational theatre with a fluid audience, loose rules about participation, and a stage that keeps changing. Learning to manage, or at least to anticipate, the actions of parties who are not at the table is critically important. In an unstable setting like ours in South Sudan, negotiators must pay attention to five types of parties not at the table:

- Parties involved in the conflict but represented by others during the negotiation;

- Organised parties who share concerns and issues with one or more of the negotiators, but who have chosen not to participate in the negotiation;

- Institutions and organisations that may be important for implementing the agreement and which may or may not have representatives at the table;

- The unorganised general public whose support for a negotiated agreement may be crucial to its success; and

- Powerful external parties not directly involved in the conflict but who can alter the negotiators' BATNA (Best Alternative to a Negotiated Agreement) by changing the context of the negotiations.

Some prior understanding are necessary. Principally, when the parties send representatives to peace talks, the negotiators are "agents" working on behalf of the "principals" in the conflict. The use of agents is a common practice in negotiations, even in stable settings. But an unstable environment increases the complexity of the relationships between agents and principals.

Any agreement made by agents must be approved by the principals, which raises questions about reliability. How accurately is each agent representing the interests and positions of his or her principal? Can any given agent "deliver" on a negotiated agreement? In other words, will behind-the-scenes negotiations validate the agreement reached at the negotiation table? Answers to these questions determine the confidence that negotiators have in their ability to reach a viable agreement, and this factor influences each party's position.

It is fundamentally important to carefully consider the above questions! Answering these questions about each agent at the peace talks can help parties to more realistically assess the risk that behind-the-scenes negotiations will derail the main negotiation:

• How formal and structured is the relationship between this agent and his or her principal(s)?

• How much legitimacy does the agent have?

Using agents need not create confusion for the negotiators. Some principal-agent relationships are formal and highly structured, as in the case of a government or rebel leadership. The relationship is administrative or professional, not personal; it is contractual as well as political. Other agents are selected through political processes that may be more or less formal and regulated. For example, an elected union representative keeps a close eye on his or her constituency so that they will not be turned out of office by the rank-and-file membership.

In an unstable setting, negotiators need to cooperatively build a unified constituency that is capable of supporting their agreement even while they are still negotiating difficult issues with one another.

Although the principal-agent relationship may be relatively formal and structured, it is messier than an attorney-client relationship. Even messier are relationships between a principal and agent when the party is a loose coalition or voluntary membership group. In groups such as a community association or an ad hoc, issue-specific activist group, membership may fluctuate so that the representative has difficulty presenting a coherent and consistent position. Furthermore, there are few, if any, formal mechanisms for the group to remove a volunteer agent from the negotiation table.

When the relationship between principal and agent is highly political or informal, it is particularly important to ascertain the agent's legitimacy. Has this agent been chosen in ways that the party considers valid and legal? Does the party believe the agent is doing a credible and acceptable job representing the party's interests and needs? An agent selected through a process deemed fair and appropriate by the party will have higher legitimacy than an agent whose selection was controversial. An agent may also gain legitimacy by succeeding in the negotiation or lose legitimacy by failing. When the party is a group rather than an individual, internal conflicts over the agent's status can disrupt the negotiations, and these should be noted, too.

Taken together, the formality of the principal-agent relationship and the agent's legitimacy among the party that he or she represents helps to determine the potential that agent-principal conflicts may disrupt inter-party negotiations.

The regulations that govern principal-agent relationships may be questioned or challenged, making it difficult to repair ruptures when they occur. And an unstable situation often produces new, loosely-organised stakeholder groups with principal-agent relationships that may be particularly difficult to manage. So, during turbulent times, we can expect to see more principal-agent relationships fragmenting.

Experience shows us that some parties can move quickly in resolving the problem at hand, while others need more time to approve or reject a proposed agreement. Parties that are capable of making quick decisions are inclined to think that other parties that need more time are stalling or negotiating in bad faith.

In conclusion, when agents are negotiating on behalf of principals, they must consult with their constituencies during negotiation. If some of the parties are not well organised, or if they are operating with cultural norms about consultation that require lengthy deliberation, the timeframe for negotiation must be adjusted accordingly. Gathering constituent views entails risks that need to be managed. Negotiators might only hear what already confirms their own view, and they might unconsciously present a distorted version of the ideas being considered by the negotiators. They can also unintentionally increase tensions among the parties if they share information in ways that damage some negotiators' standing with other stakeholder groups.

In the best practice of negotiation, an inclusive demonstration must be upheld. To check the validity of information that has been gathered informally, negotiators can convene more formal meetings, such as public feedback sessions involving representatives from multiple stakeholders. When doing this, negotiators should think carefully about how to share information in ways that don't incite resistance to the negotiation process. A facilitator with no personal interest in the negotiation can help structure the information gathering and information sharing processes to elicit open-ended, creative, and non-judgemental responses. Using a facilitator also allows the negotiators to listen attentively to the participants' ideas.

Peace Talks Must Negotiate Meaning

First and foremost, I believe that the broader peace process is meant for the whole country, even though the majority of the nation may not fully grasp the core of the matters at hand. Therefore, to negotiate issues, the parties need to have a coordinated or shared sense of their context. In stable times, the shared sense of reality is enacted through institutions such as the courts, schools, the political system, local elders, and bureaucracies. In times of turbulence, which are often brought on by changes that destabilise existing social systems, the parties do not have an adequate enough sense of a shared context to support negotiation. The structures that are meant to create a shared sense of meaning may be broken or missing; they can no longer function because they do not have adequate support from the citizenry or because they literally have been destroyed.

The truth of the matter is here! Missing or broken systems cannot be imposed on people; rather, they must be renegotiated and revalidated by the people. This is a challenge of creating meaning. In our South Sudan reality, the context of our negotiations is unstable in large measure because the parties give different meanings to their shared environment and to their relationships. Some people talk about parties in conflict having different perceptions or different worldviews. Perceptions and worldviews are not the same thing, and the differences between them are important.

More precisely, differences in worldviews are particularly difficult to navigate. Such differences require careful attention to the ways people construct their senses of reality. What is our sense of reality as South Sudanese? It is helpful to think about people as world-viewing beings. World-viewing is an active process of creating meaning. Everyone engages in world-viewing, but our world-viewing activities are largely unconscious, and our own worldview is so intrinsic and common sense to us that we only become aware of it when we encounter someone who does not share our worldview.

It is purely common sense, we cannot easily answer the question, "What is your worldview?" However, our worldviews are revealed in our language, attitudes, manners, and behaviours. They are particularly evident in the stories we tell about our lives and about the world around us. In our storytelling and our actions, we indirectly answer five questions:

• What is real? Or what is really the cause of this or that?

• How is our world organised?

• What do we value and not value in our world?

• What constitutes real knowledge in our world?

• How should we (and others) act in our world?

Worldviews are not infinitely flexible, but neither are they fixed and absolute. They contain uncertainties and internal inconsistencies, and they change in response to shifting circumstances, including encounters with others who do not share the same worldview.

Reading more deeply into the violence that has eroded South Sudan for decades, we can see that differing worldviews are at the root of our disagreements. Unstable settings expose the uncertainties, inconsistencies, and conflicts in the parties' world-viewing, and this forces everyone to expend energy on making sense of the five world-viewing questions listed above. Therefore, people must spend more time than usual on storytelling and other activities that help them to create a sense of reality that is adequately shared, in order to allow for joint action in the world, including the joint action of negotiation.

For sure, in many unstable settings, the parties' competing senses of reality are among the root causes of their conflict. They may not even recognise this difference until they start telling their stories in the presence of another person who can help them assess their lives. Parties in a conflict may even do world-viewing in ways that exclude or make invisible some parts of reality.

In unstable settings, the parties need to identify and wrestle with their differences in worldviews in order to create a sense of a shared reality that can sustain new relationships and new ways of living together. The traditional rational-analytical processes of negotiation and the instrumental and relational language of negotiation are not adequate for creating shared meanings. Stories must be told, listened to deeply, and new, shared stories must be created if the parties are going to achieve a stable sense of reality that accommodates a peaceful future.

Telling My Story in Negotiation

Space must be created for any party to the conflict to tell his or her story in a clear and conducive manner. Telling one's story enters any negotiation when the parties to the conflict use persuasion to make their case for a particular agreement. For example, Party A says, "Because the world is this way and our relationship is like this, then you should do X." Party B counters with an alternate story about reality and a different suggested outcome. In spite of this, few negotiators focus on the nature of the stories that people tell during the negotiation process and the way that these stories may shape the negotiation process. Little attention has also been given to the ways in which negotiators can combine processes of shared storytelling (renegotiating reality) and problem-solving (negotiating issues).

Complex multiparty stakeholders negotiations, such as those between warring parties, may be preceded or accompanied by processes for building positive relationships among the parties. This creates some opportunity to negotiate reality, but the possibilities are limited since creating meaning is about more than just building positive relationships; it is also about building a shared story about our world that can include all of the parties in ways they find meaningful and appropriate. For example, one usually unspoken story that influences political negotiation is the story of human beings as being made in the image of God and being co-creators of the world. This story makes it difficult to raise issues of values, ethics, and meaning that might envision another relationship between nature and human communities. The parties can spend time together and build positive interpersonal relationships, but if they don't focus on creating a story that embraces other possible relationships between human beings and their nation or nature, they will have a hard time negotiating intractable political conflicts.

Once negotiated agreement is reached, it then becomes our storytelling point; it embodies new ways of talking about and acting in the world and it accepts a limited array of possible relationships among parties. As with any world-naming story, it can exclude or include others. Because all the parties involved in the conflict are not at the table, the negotiators can easily fall into a trap of creating a shared narrative that displaces the blame for their current situation and loads the cost of fixing the problem onto a party not participating in the negotiation. Negotiators need to remember that the parties they are blaming are part of the "audience" that needs to validate and support the agreement. Therefore, displacing blame for the problem, and the burden for fixing it, onto others is a recipe for failure.

It is also obvious that when not enough attention is being paid to storytelling, stories may become distorted. Even if blame is not displaced, others will experience the world- naming story of a negotiated agreement as an attempt to reshape their reality and control their options in life. They may embrace this story, or they may reject it, particularly if they are not "in" the story or if they think enacting the story will cause harm to them or to things and people they cherish. Their resistance can take the form of lawsuits, protests, media campaigns, or even violence.

In conclusion, it is wise to say that time must be spent and awareness must be created to see that stories are told in an honest manner! Surely, when doing this kind of exploration, it is helpful if the negotiators can carve out a time and place for the free flow of creativity, without judgement or risk of getting trapped into an agreement or commitment. This can be done with brainstorming sessions, visioning activities, role-playing (parties take on the roles of others in the conflict), and other creative learning activities.

It is useful to mark these times clearly as "not negotiating" so that the parties can participate freely and creatively. Literally moving to a different location and setting the furniture in the room differently can help free participants from the mind-set of negotiating. Getting a facilitator to help with the process can also change the parties' understanding of what they are doing. The key to success, however, is finding ways to engage participants in creative conversations, that invites the participants to shift the way they view themselves, others, and their problem.

Owning and Accepting the Agreement

The most difficult stage is to sustain and own a negotiated agreement once it has been signed. Efforts must be made to sustain the agreement in its signed form. For example, let's assume that the negotiators in our South Sudan case have reached an agreement. Now what happens? That depends on the support systems that exist and on the support that negotiators can win from those who were not involved in the negotiation. If support systems are missing or lack legitimacy, then the negotiators will need to sell the agreement to others, especially those at the grassroots. This is not an either/or situation; rather, it is a matter of degree. Even if support mechanisms such as government institutions or courts are fully functional, the parties may need to build political support so that other parties don't prevent the ratification and implementation of the negotiated agreement.

Carrying out the agreement relies heavily on the ability of the government and other national institutions or agencies to sustain a commitment to the project. If the general public mobilises against the project, government or agency officials may end the project. This is where wooing public support is particularly important, but the negotiators may not see that so clearly.

Sadly, there are also instances where agreed negotiated agreements are not given support at all. Having worked hard to craft an agreement on difficult issues, negotiators are frequently surprised when others resist their proposed plans, and they often are unprepared to manage the negative responses. Before doubting the merits of their work or getting angry with others for being uncooperative, negotiators must consider the environment in which they are working. Negative responses may not be reactions to the proposal as much as they are expressions of frustration with a world that feels chaotic.

Negotiated agreements may have drastic or dramatic changes on people's lives, and may affect them forever, so efforts must be made to assist people in accepting changes. For example, the following factors influence the way people respond to change:

- Did they choose the change or was it imposed on them?
- Did they anticipate the change or was it unexpected?
- Is the change seen as a minor inconvenience or a major disruptive force?
- Does the change feel positive or negative to them?

It is equally important to spend time deciding how to best sell the negotiated agreement and determine how it will be implemented. If negotiators understand and work with these realities, they can introduce the changes that they are proposing in ways that maximise the potential for support.

Working with Public Resistance

In unstable settings, the negotiators lack the capacity and legitimacy to make others cooperate with their plans, and the institutions that might otherwise enforce an agreement are too unstable to fulfil that role.

Therefore, the negotiators must take responsibility for building the political will and for promoting institutional mechanisms to support and sustain newly negotiated cooperative relationships. Exactly how much an agreement depends on political support from the public must be determined case by case. In some situations, just getting the public not to protest or resist an agreement is adequate, whereas in other situations, the public must actively cooperate to implement the agreement.

Secrecy is antithetical to the process of building political will. However, many negotiators think that secrecy is necessary to get their work done, and they are right in some ways. You can't do hard negotiating and problem-solving with television cameras tracking your every move. In strategic negotiations, finding the balance between sharing information to prepare the public for an agreement, and creating the space for negotiators to take risks and be creative is a delicate balance.

Faced with the dilemma of how much information should be shared with the public, negotiators must deftly navigate the sensitive digital world in which we live and work. When thinking about how much information to release publicly, negotiators should consider at least two factors:

- How significantly will the negotiated outcome affect the general public?
- How much public support will be necessary to implement the negotiated agreement?

Methods in Training the Public

It is not always an easy job to prepare citizens for peace and reconciliation after peace negotiation without entering into confrontation. As a matter of fact, to find the balance between secrecy and transparency, the negotiators need a shared map of the overall situation. Even if they do not reach complete agreement on this map, they can still use it to make plans for managing the behind-the-scenes interactions needed to support their work. They can also revisit the map periodically to make sense of contextual changes that develop during their negotiations.

As they build their map, and later as they craft an agreement, the negotiators need to think about how much public support will be required to implement their agreement. Does their agreement need voter approval? Does it need citizen cooperation? Does it expect people to change their behaviours? Does it simply need public tolerance rather than active support? Does it require the support of powerful actors such as parliament, the president, IGAD or other international actors?

While working through problems and building support among organised stakeholder groups who are not at the table, the negotiators should also think about how much information they need to share with the public, when to share the information, and how best to share it. The larger the impact that a negotiated agreement will have on the general public, the more transparent the negotiations need to be. People change more readily if they understand why a change is needed, if they see the change coming, and if they feel they had some input into the ways the change will be implemented. Similarly, the more the agreement depends on active support from the public, the more the negotiators need to educate and prepare the public to understand and accept the agreement.

Educating the public requires much more than periodic announcements that the negotiations are going well or floating proposed agreements to see how the public responds. Strategies that negotiators might consider for keeping the public informed about their work include:

- Have stakeholder groups who are not at the table educate their constituents about the positive work being done;
- Get normally hostile stakeholder groups to make a joint statement of support for the negotiation process;
- Prepare joint press releases about the negotiation and invite feedback from the public;
- Make sure the general public is aware of public feedback meetings and structure those meetings so that persons not tied to stakeholder groups can participate; and
- Invite media to do in-depth stories about the issues being negotiated in order to increase public awareness of the problems the negotiators are addressing.

Realistic Approach to the Agreement

For obvious reasons, people engaged in the activities of pursuing peace are hugely stressed and exhausted when an agreement is finally reached. The negotiators are also tired. They probably don't have the energy to implement the agreement, and they are often not the correct people for that job. If they have done their work well and brought others into the negotiation as consultants or shadow negotiators, they can hand the process of executing the agreement to others. At the same time, the negotiators, or perhaps another oversight group created as part of the negotiated agreement, need to be prepared to revisit issues and renegotiate unanticipated problems as they arise. Mobilising resources for sustaining the agreement must continue, because you never know for sure that the agreement will hold permanently, peace is elusive.

While I have been participating in the peace talks for South Sudan, I believe that I am coming to full terms with myself as to how difficult and expensive peace negotiations can be. Really, implementing agreements in complex cases is a long-term undertaking that involves mobilising resources and coordinating the activities of multiple organisations and actors. Everyone else will need the support of various different parties who were not in the primary negotiation. The more a settlement depends on resources that are not controlled by the parties at the table, the greater the need for negotiators to work throughout the negotiation process on behind-the-scenes discussions to mobilise those resources. Creating a shared vision and shared realistic plans for mobilising resources is an important part of strategic negotiation in unstable settings.

Creating Visionary Leadership

The signed negotiated agreement should be implemented to the letter. A visionary and consistent leadership is crucial to long-term sustainability of the nation once agreement is reached. In fact, when there are few stable institutions to support a negotiated agreement, visionary leadership is critically important. Honestly speaking, negotiators and citizens need to think about cultivating visionary leadership at all levels of the system in which they are working. Again, this is part of the behind-the-scenes discussion process during negotiation, and it is a significant factor in the success of an agreement.

The biggest temptation for South Sudanese is how to decide wisely whom they want to lead them, and also for them to put their trust into a particular leadership established to lead them to the promised future. Obviously, the biggest challenge is creating a sense of shared leadership. In times of turmoil, people often look for strong leaders who can "fix things." Insofar as the negotiators have taken on the role of community leaders in order to cultivate support for the agreement, others may want them to remain in leadership roles or assume more responsibility for the long-term success of the agreement than is realistic. If the negotiators have identified leaders throughout the system, invited them into the negotiation process through behind-the-table consultations, and garnered their support for the agreement, then the negotiators can feel more confident that others will put energy into making the agreement a reality.

Educating the Public about the Agreement

The real time of truth comes with the presentation of the negotiated agreement to the public. A lot is expected from the team to do the job credibly well. When introducing their agreement, negotiators need to be clear about what they have and have not negotiated. Otherwise, many people will expect more than is realistic from the agreement. They should also help people understand how this small agreement will help promote long-term changes for the better. Here, the negotiators do well to remember that they are inviting people into a new story; they are not presenting a list of rational, logical steps that people will follow because they make sense. People act out of their stories more than their sense of logic. They need to see and feel how this agreement opens new possibilities for a better life.

Negotiators should ponder carefully who makes the announcement of the agreement. Clearly, they need to own their work. But their work may have a better chance of succeeding if they share the limelight with others less involved in the negotiation, particularly if they can get a coalition of normally-hostile groups who were not at the table to stand with them in support of the agreement.

Resiliency as a Prerequisite for Planning

When I caution for prudency and serious resilience of spirit, I am speaking both to South Sudan and also myself in the company of the people who are negotiating peace for South Sudan. This cardinal element was forgotten in our previous agreements! The turbulent environment we have in our nation today means that any negotiated agreement reached is going to encounter difficulties and setbacks.

Negotiators and all stakeholders can prepare for this by building into the negotiated agreement mechanisms for renegotiating the agreement, if necessary, when problems occur. When presenting the agreement, the fact that setbacks will occur should be openly acknowledged.

Then when the first obstacles are encountered, the negotiators can help immensely if they stand united in their commitment to the agreement, normalise the difficulties, and provide leadership for getting through the problem. Negotiators can bring about positive social changes in the midst of what feels like chaos to many people. Such courage will help to establish an authentic and credible authority to enhance accountability, transparency, reparation and restoration.

CHAPTER FOUR

Restorative Justice: A New Vocabulary

In this chapter, I would like to present the concept of restorative justice. There cannot be a quick fix to the problems that have brought about the need for reconciliation in our nation without a close examination of restoration justice, or 'healing'.

How should we as a society respond to wrongdoing? When a crime occurs or an injustice is done, what needs to happen? What does justice require?

The South Sudanese criminal justice system's approach to justice has some important strengths, but there remains huge room for development and improvement. Yet there is also a growing acknowledgment of this system's serious limits and failures. Victims, offenders, and community members often feel that justice does not adequately meet their needs. Justice professionals – judges, lawyers, prosecutors, probation and parole officers, and prison staff – frequently express a sense of frustration as well. Many feel that the process of justice deepens societal wounds and conflicts rather than contributing to healing or peace.

Restorative justice began as an effort to deal with burglary and other property crimes that are usually viewed (often incorrectly) as relatively minor offenses. Today, however, restorative approaches are available in some communities for the most severe forms of criminal violence: death caused by drunken driving, assault, rape, and murder. Building upon the experience of the Truth and Reconciliation Commission in South Africa, efforts are also being made to apply a restorative justice framework to situations of mass violence.

These approaches and practices are also spreading beyond the criminal justice system to schools, to the workplace, and to religious institutions. Some advocate the use of restorative approaches such as "circles" (a particular practice that emerged from First Nation communities in Canada) as a way to work through, resolve, and transform conflicts in general. Others pursue circles or "conferences" as a way to build and heal communities

Kay Pranis, a prominent restorative justice advocate, calls circles a form of participatory democracy that moves beyond simple majority rule.

Our nation is under pressure from the international community and international agencies to adhere only to the Western way of problem-solving, thereby seriously neglecting our traditional justice systems. Where Western legal systems are gradually suppressing and/or replacing traditional justice and conflict-resolution processes, restorative justice, together with the South Sudanese traditional justice systems, can provide a framework to reexamine and sometimes reactivate these traditions.

Although the term "restorative justice" encompasses a variety of programmes and practices, at its core it is a set of principles, a philosophy, an alternate set of guiding questions. Ultimately, restorative justice provides an alternative framework for thinking about wrongdoing.

Why Restorative Justice?

First and foremost, in this chapter, I do not try to make the case for restorative justice. Nor do I explore the many implications of the restorative justice approach. Rather, I intend this chapter to be a brief description or overview to help in our case for reconciliation and healing for the people of South Sudan. Although I will outline some of the programmes and practices of restorative justice, my focus in this chapter is on the principles and philosophy of restorative justice, and how it relates to reconciliation.

I hope to help bring clarity about where the restorative justice "train" should be headed and, in some cases, to nudge the train back onto the track.

Such an effort is important at this time. Like all attempts at change, restorative justice has sometimes lost its way as it has developed and spread. With more and more programmes being termed "restorative justice," the meaning of that phrase is sometimes diluted or confused. Under the inevitable pressures of working in real world circumstances, restorative justice has sometimes been subtly coopted or diverted from its principles.

The victim advocacy community has been especially concerned about this. Restorative justice claims to be victim-oriented, but is it really? All too often, victim groups fear that restorative justice efforts are motivated mainly by a desire to work with offenders in a more positive way. Like the criminal system that it aims to improve or replace, restorative justice may become primarily a way to deal with offenders, largely ignoring victims in the process.

Others wonder whether the process has adequately addressed offenders' needs and made sufficiently restorative efforts. Do restorative justice programmes give adequate support to offenders to carry out their obligations and to change their patterns of behaviour? Do the programmes adequately address the harm that may have led offenders to become who they are? Are such programmes becoming just another way to punish offenders under a new guise? And what about the community at large? Is the community being adequately encouraged to be involved and to assume its obligations to victims, to offenders, and to its members in general?

I must acknowledge certain limits to the framework I will lay out here. Even though I will try as hard as I can to remain critical and open, I come with bias in favour of this ideal. Moreover, in spite of all efforts to the contrary, I write from my own perspective, which is shaped by who I am: a South Sudanese from Western Equatoria, a Christian, a Catholic, a member of the clergy and a Bishop. My personal background, as well as my interests and other factors, necessarily shape my voice and vision.

Even though there is somewhat of a consensus within the field about the broad outline of the principles of restorative justice, not all that follows is uncontested. What you read here is my understanding of restorative justice. It must be tested against the voices of others.

Misrepresentation of Restorative Justice

Restorative justice is not primarily about forgiveness or reconciliation. Some victims and victim advocates react negatively to restorative justice because they imagine that the goal of such programmes is to encourage them, or even to coerce them, to forgive or reconcile with offenders.

As we shall see, forgiveness and reconciliation are not primary principles of restorative justice. It is true that restorative justice does provide a context where either or both might happen. Indeed, some degree of forgiveness, or even reconciliation, does occur much more frequently under restorative justice than in the adversarial setting of the criminal justice system. However, this is a choice that is entirely up to the participants. There should be no pressure to choose to forgive or to seek reconciliation.

Restorative Justice Is Not Mediation

Like mediation programmes, many restorative justice programmes are designed around the possibility of a facilitated meeting or an encounter between victims, offenders, and perhaps community members. However, an encounter is not always chosen or even appropriate in the circumstances.

Moreover, restorative justice approaches are important even when an offender has not been apprehended or when a party is unwilling or unable to meet. So, restorative justice approaches are not limited to only encounters, there are also other possibilities.

Even when an encounter occurs, the term "mediation" is not a fitting description of what could happen. In a mediated conflict or dispute, parties are assumed to be on a level moral playing field, often with responsibilities that may need to be shared on all sides. While this sense of shared blame may be true in some criminal cases, in many cases it is not. In fact, those involved may well be struggling to overcome a tendency to blame themselves.

At any rate, to participate in most restorative justice encounters, a wrongdoer must admit to some level of responsibility for the offence, and an important component of such programmes is to name and acknowledge the wrongdoing. The neutral language of mediation may be misleading and even offensive in many cases.

Restorative Justice Is Concerned about Needs and Roles

Restorative justice is an effort to rethink the needs brought about when crimes are committed, as well as the roles implicit in crimes. Restorative justice expands the circle of stakeholders (those with a stake or standing in the event or the case) beyond just the government and the offender to include victims and community members.

Victims

Of special concern with restorative justice are the needs of victims; more specifically, the needs of victims that are not being adequately met by the criminal justice system. Victims often feel ignored, neglected, or even abused by the justice process. They often have a number of specific needs from the justice process which seem to be especially neglected:

- *Information*: Victims need answers to questions that they have about the offence: why it happened and what has happened since. They need real information, not speculation or the legally constrained information that comes from a trial or plea agreement. Securing real information usually requires direct or indirect access to offenders who hold this information.

- *Truth-telling*: An important element in healing or transcending the experience of crime is an opportunity to tell the story of what happened. There are good therapeutic reasons for this. Part of the trauma of crime is the way it upsets our views of ourselves and our world, our life-stories. Transcendence of these experiences means "restoring" our lives by telling the stories in significant settings, often where they can receive public acknowledgment. Often, too, it is important for victims to tell their stories to the ones who caused them harm and to have them understand the impact of their actions.

- *Empowerment*: Victims often feel that control has been taken away from them by the offences they've experienced. They've lost control over their properties, their bodies, their emotions, and their dreams. Involvement in their own cases as they go through the justice process can be an important way to return a sense of empowerment to them.

- *Restitution or vindication*; Restitution by offenders is often important to victims, sometimes because of the actual losses, but just as importantly, because of the symbolic recognition and restoration of human dignity that restitution implies. When an offender makes an effort to rectify the harm that he or she has caused, even if only partially, it is a way of saying, "I am taking responsibility, and you are not to blame."

A major area of concern that gave rise to restorative justice is offender accountability. The criminal justice system is concerned about holding offenders accountable, but that means making sure offenders get the punishment they deserve. Little in the process encourages offenders to understand the consequences of their actions on their victims, or to empathise with their victims. On the contrary, the adversarial game requires offenders to look out for themselves. Offenders are discouraged from acknowledging their responsibility and are given little opportunity to act on this responsibility in concrete ways.

The neutralising strategies (the stereotypes and rationalisations that offenders often use to distance themselves from the people they have hurt) are never challenged. Unfortunately, then, an offender's sense of alienation from society is only heightened by the legal process and by the prison experience. For a variety of reasons, the legal process tends to discourage responsibility and empathy on the part of offenders.

Restorative justice has brought an awareness of the limits and negative byproducts of retributive punishment. Beyond that, however, it has argued that punishment is not real accountability. Real accountability involves facing up to what one has done. It means encouraging offenders to understand the impact of their behaviour and the harms that they have caused, and urges them to take steps to put things right as much as possible. This accountability, it is argued, is better for victims, better for society, and better for offenders.

Offenders

Offenders have other needs beyond their responsibilities to victims and communities. If we expect them to assume their responsibilities, to change their behaviour, to become contributing members of our communities, their needs, according to restorative justice, must also be addressed. That subject is beyond the scope of this chapter, but the following suggests some things that offenders need from justice:

- Accountability that addresses the resulting harm, encourages empathy and responsibility, and transforms shame;
- Encouragement to experience personal transformation, including healing for the harm that contributed to their offending behaviour, opportunities for treatment for addictions and/or other problems, enhancement of personal competencies;
- Encouragement and support for integration into the community; and
- For some, at least temporary restraint.

Communities

Community members have needs arising from crime, too, and they also have roles to play. Communities are impacted by crime, and in many cases should be considered stakeholders, as secondary victims. Community members can become involved in a case, and can initiate a forum to work on these matters, while strengthening the community itself. The following list suggests some areas of concern for communities as far as their justice needs are concerned:

- Attention to their concerns as victims;
- Opportunities to build a sense of community and mutual account-ability; and
- Encouragement to take on their obligations for the welfare of their members, including victims and offenders, and to foster the conditions that promote healthy communities.

In short, the legal or criminal justice system centres around offenders and focuses on making sure that offenders get what they deserve in terms of punishment. Restorative justice, on the other hand, is more focused on needs: those of victims, of communities, and of offenders.

Restorative Principles

Restorative justice is based on an old, common sense understanding of wrongdoing. Although it would be expressed differently in different cultures, this approach is probably common to most traditional societies. For those of us from a South Sudanese background, it is the way many of our ancestors (and perhaps even our parents) understood wrongdoing:

- Crime is a violation of people and of interpersonal relationships; and
- Violations create obligations.The central obligation is to put right the wrongs committed.

Underlying this understanding of wrongdoing is an assumption about society: that we are all interconnected. In the Hebrew Scriptures, this is embedded in the concept of shalom, the vision of living in a sense of 'all-rightness' with each other, with the creator, and with the environment. Many cultures have a word that represents this: *jo* or *hozho*; and, for many Africans, the Bantu word *ubuntu*. Although the specific meanings of these words vary, they communicate a similar message: all things are connected to each other in a web of relationships.

The problem that crime creates, in this worldview, is that it wounds the community and it tears the web of relationships. Crime represents damaged relationships. In fact, damaged relationships are both a cause and an effect of crime. Many traditions have a saying that the harm of one is the harm of all, that a harm such as crime ripples out to disrupt the whole web. Moreover, wrongdoing is often a symptom that something is out of balance in the web.

Inter-relationships imply mutual obligations and responsibilities. I comes as no surprise, then, that this view of wrongdoing emphasises the importance of making amends or "putting right". Indeed, making amends for wrongdoing is an obligation. While the initial emphasis may be on the obligations owed by offenders, the focus on interconnectedness opens the possibility that others (especially the larger community) may have obligations as well. Even more fundamentally, this view of wrongdoing implies a concern for the healing of those involved – victims, but also offenders and broader communities.

In an often-quoted passage from Christian and Jewish Scripture, the prophet Micah asks the question, "What does the Lord require?" The answer begins with the phrase, "to do justice." But what does justice require? The legal system's answer has focused on making sure offenders get what they deserve. Restorative justice answers this question differently, focusing first of all on needs and associated obligations.

Criminal Justice Versus Restorative Justice

We will now look at the different views presented by criminal justice and restorative justice.

Criminal justice presents its concerns as follows:

- Crime is a violation of the law and the state;
- Violations create guilt;
- Justice requires the state to determine blame (guilt) and impose pain (punishment); and
- The central focus is on giving offenders what they deserve.

Restorative justice presents its concerns as follows:

- Crime is a violation of people and relationships;
- Violations create obligations;
- Justice involves victims, offenders, and community members, who must come together in an effort to put things right; and
- The central focus is on victims' needs and offender responsibility for repairing harm.

Criminal justice asks the following questions:

- What laws have been broken?
- Who did it?
- What do they deserve?

Whereas restorative justice asks:
- Who has been hurt?
- What are their needs?
- Whose obligations are these?

The Three Pillars of Restorative Justice

Three central concepts, or pillars, deserve a closer look: harms and needs, obligations, and engagement.

1. Restorative justice focuses on harm

Restorative justice understands crime, first of all, as harm done to people and communities. Our legal system, with its focus on rules and laws, and with its view that the state is the victim, often loses sight of this reality.

Concerned primarily with making sure that offenders get what they deserve, the legal system considers victims, at best, a secondary concern of justice. Focusing on the harm committed, on the contrary, implies an inherent concern for victims' needs and roles.

For restorative justice, then, justice begins with a concern for victims and their needs. It seeks to repair the harm as much as possible, both concretely and symbolically. This victim-oriented approach requires that justice be concerned about victims' needs even when no offender has been identified or apprehended.

While our first concern must be the harm experienced by victims, the focus on harm implies that we also need to be concerned about the harm experienced by offenders and communities. This may require us to address the root causes of crime. The goal of restorative justice is to provide an experience of healing for *all* parties concerned, not just victims.

2. Wrongs or harms result in obligations

Therefore, restorative justice emphasises offender accountability and responsibility. The legal system defines accountability as making sure offenders are punished. If crime is essentially about harm, however, accountability means offenders must be encouraged to understand that harm. Offenders must begin to comprehend the consequences of their behaviour. Moreover, it means they have a responsibility to make things right as much as possible, both concretely and symbolically.

As we shall see, the first obligation is the offender's, but the community and society have obligations as well.

3. Restorative justice promotes engagement or participation

The principle of engagement suggests that the primary parties affected by crime (victims, offenders, members of the community) are given significant roles in the justice process. These stakeholders need to be given information about each other and they need to be involved in deciding what justice requires in each case.

In some cases, this may mean actual dialogue between these parties, as happens in victim-offender encounters. They would share their stories and come to a consensus about what should be done. In other cases, it may involve indirect exchanges, the use of surrogates, or other forms of involvement.

The principle of engagement implies involvement of an enlarged circle of parties as compared to the traditional justice process.

So restorative justice is constructed upon three simple elements or pillars:

- Harms and related needs (of victims, first of all, but also of the communities and the offenders);
- Obligations that have resulted from (and given rise to) this harm (the offenders', but also the communities'); and
- Engagement of those who have a legitimate interest or stake in the offence and its resolution (victims, offenders, and community members).

Here, in summary is a skeletal outline of restorative justice. Although it is inadequate by itself, it provides a framework upon which a fuller understanding can be built.

Restorative justice requires, at minimum, that we address victims' harms and needs, hold offenders accountable to put right those harms, and involve victims, offenders and communities in this process.

The "who" and the "how" are important. Who is involved in the justice process, and how they are involved, are important elements of restorative justice. We will now examine these aspects in more depth.

Process – the "how": Our legal (criminal justice) system is an adversarial process that is conducted by professionals who stand in for the offender and the state, with matters being refereed by a judge. Outcomes are imposed by an authority (the law, judges, juries) who stand outside the essential conflict. Victims, community members, even offenders, rarely participate in this process in any substantial way.

On the other hand, although restorative justice usually recognises the need for outside authorities and, in some cases, imposed outcomes, it prefers processes that are collaborative and inclusive and, to the greatest extent possible, outcomes that are mutually agreed upon rather than imposed.

Restorative justice usually acknowledges that there is a place for the adversarial approach and the role of professionals, and also recognises an important role for the state. However, restorative justice prefers inclusive, collaborative processes and consensual outcomes.

A direct, facilitated, face-to-face encounter – with adequate screening, preparation, and safeguards – is often an ideal forum for the participation of stakeholders in restorative justice. As we shall see shortly, this can take a variety of forms, including a meeting between victim and offender, a family group conference, or a circle process.

A meeting allows a victim and an offender to put a face to each other, to ask questions of each other directly, to negotiate together how to put things right. It provides an opportunity for victims to tell offenders directly the impact of the offence or to ask questions. It allows offenders to hear and to begin to understand the consequences of their behaviour. It offers possibilities for acceptance of responsibility and apology. Many victims and offenders have found such a meeting to be a powerful and positive experience.

An encounter, either direct or indirect, is not always possible, and, in some cases, may not be desirable. In some cultures, a direct encounter may be inappropriate. An indirect encounter that may be reasonably effective but not offensive might include a letter or a video exchange. Restorative justice emphasises the importance of participation by those who have a direct stake in the event or offence, that is, those who are involved or impacted or a person who represents the victim. In all cases, efforts should be made to provide maximum exchange of information between stakeholders and to secure the maximum involvement of such stakeholders.

Stakeholders – the "who": The key stakeholders, of course, are the immediate victims and offenders. Members of the community may be directly affected and thus should also be considered immediate stakeholders. In addition to this circle, there are others who have varying degrees of stake in the situation. These may include family members, friends, or other "secondary victims" such as offenders' families or friends, or other members of the community.

It may be helpful to differentiate between "community" and "society." Restorative justice has tended to focus on the micro-communities of place or relationships that are directly affected by an offence, but which are often neglected by "state justice." However, there are larger concerns and obligations that belong to society beyond those stakeholders who have a direct interest in a particular event. These include a society's concern for the safety, human rights, and the general wellbeing of its members. Many argue that the government has an important and legitimate role in looking after such societal concerns.

Central to restorative justice is the idea of making things right or, to use a more active phrase often used in British English, "putting right". As already noted, this implies a responsibility on the part of the offender to, as much as possible, take active steps to repair the harm to the victim (and perhaps the impacted community). In cases such as murder, the harm obviously cannot be repaired; however, symbolic steps, including acknowledgment of responsibility or restitution, can be helpful to victims and are the responsibility of offenders.

Putting right implies reparation or restoration or recovery, but these "re"-words are often inadequate. When a severe wrong has been committed, there is no possibility of repairing the harm or going back to what was before.

It is possible that a victim can be helped towards healing when an offender works towards making things right, whether actually or symbolically. Many victims, however, are ambivalent about the term "healing," because of the sense of finality or termination that it connotes. This journey belongs to victims (no one else can do it for them), but an effort to put right can assist in this process, although it can never fully restore.

The obligation to put right is first of all the offender's, but the community may have responsibilities as well – to the victim, but perhaps also to the offender. For offenders to successfully carry out their obligations, they may need support and encouragement from the wider community. Moreover, the community has responsibilities for the situations that are causing or encouraging crime. Ideally, restorative justice processes can provide a catalyst and/or a forum for exploring and assigning these needs, responsibilities, and expectations.

Addressing Causes

Putting right requires that we address both the harm and also the causes of crime. Most victims want this. They want to know that steps are being taken to reduce such harm to themselves and others.

Offenders have an obligation to address the causes of their behaviour, but they usually cannot do this alone. There may be larger obligations beyond those of offenders – for example, the social injustices and other conditions that cause crime or create unsafe conditions. Many times, others in addition to the offenders have responsibilities as well: families, the larger community, and society as a whole.

If we are to address harm and causes, we must also explore the harm that offenders themselves have experienced. Many offenders have themselves been victimised or traumatised in significant ways. Many other offenders perceive themselves to have been victimised. These perceptions may be an important contributing cause of crime. In fact, Harvard professor and former prison psychiatrist, James Gilligan, has argued that all violence is an effort to achieve justice or to undo injustice. In other words, much crime may be a response to – an effort to undo as such – a sense of victimisation.

A perception of oneself as victim does not absolve responsibility for offending behaviour. However, if Gilligan is right, neither can we expect offending behaviour to stop without addressing this sense of victimisation. In fact, punishment often reinforces the sense of victimisation. Sometimes offenders are satisfied when their sense of being victims is simply acknowledged. Sometimes their perception of being victims must be challenged. Sometimes the damage done must be repaired before offenders can be expected to change their behaviour.

Trauma is a core experience not only of victims, but also of many offenders. Much violence may actually be a reenactment of trauma that offenders experienced years earlier, but which was not responded to adequately. Society tends to respond by delivering more trauma in the form of imprisonment. While the realities of trauma must not be used to excuse, they must be understood, and they must be addressed.

In summary, an effort to put right the wrongs committed is the core of restorative justice. Putting right has two dimensions:

- Addressing the harm that has been done, and
- Addressing the causes of that harm.

Restorative justice is ultimately concerned about the restoration and reintegration of both victims and offenders, in addition to the wellbeing of the entire community. Restorative justice is about balancing concern for all parties. Restorative justice encourages outcomes that promote responsibility, reparation, and healing for all.

The Goals of Restorative Justice

In her excellent handbook, *Restorative Justice: A Vision for Healing and Change*, Susan Sharper summarised the goals and tasks of restorative justice in this way:

Restorative justice programmes aim to:

• Put key decisions into the hands of those most affected by crime;

• Make justice more healing and, ideally, more transformative; and

• Reduce the likelihood of future offences.

Achieving these goals requires that:

• Victims are involved in the process and come out of it satisfied;

• Offenders understand how their actions have affected other people and take responsibility for those actions;

• Outcomes help to repair the harm done and address the reasons for the offence (specific plans are tailored to the victim's and the offender's needs), and victim and offender both gain a sense of "closure," and both are reintegrated into the community.

True justice requires, instead, that we ask questions such as these: Who has been hurt? What do they need? Whose obligations and responsibilities are these? Who has a stake in this situation? What is the process that can involve the stakeholders in finding a solution? Consequently, restorative justice requires us to change not just our lenses, but also our questions.

Above all, restorative justice is an invitation to join in conversation so that we may support and learn from each other. It is a reminder that all of us are indeed interconnected which is the sure catalyst for reconciliation and healing.

CHAPTER FIVE

Reconciliation:
A Gift from God for Humanity

Restoring the Humanity of Victims

This fifth chapter makes the project of our book complete and fulfilled. At the end of chapter four, we saw how much the notion of reconciliation may differ according to circumstances. Here I wish to examine the perceptions of violence and how to acquire the habit of getting rid of them.

Rene Girard, an anthropologist has said that:

Violence lies at the formation of every culture or society. That violence explains why every society is inherently unstable and why societies resort to violence as a way of handling conflict.[41]

Although this understanding does not provide enough information on what violence really is, by looking at our society we can tell how our weaker being and nature prevails. There is a lot of fear in each person indicating the background of his personal formation. If the society is aware of its fragility, then there is an intense need to develop maximum attention and defence. It is the duty of each and every individual to rebuild a true sense of security and dignity.

This kind of habit is what Schreiter refers to as the construction of human meaning, which embraces all that is around him:

It is our symbolmaking activities that give us the capacity to construct those senses of safety and selfhood. They do this by assigning meaning to both the physical features and the temporal events in our lives. These meanings give our lives definition, a sense of sameness that reassures us of who we are and how we fit into things. That reassurance gives us a certain sense of safety that permits us to shift our attention elsewhere. That sense of sameness, which grows out of those clutches of meaning, gives rise to our definition of us as selves. Our selfhood in turn guides us

---

[41] RENÉ GIRARD, *Violence and the Sacred,* Baltimore 1977, pp. 1-2.

through the flow of time. It becomes a point of reference, providing us a sense of location and orientation in the flow of time.[42]

Throughout the chapters of this book, we have been repeatedly referring to violence and suffering in short or brief descriptions of what South Sudanese have experienced. The people went through many upheavals in the various circumstances of their violence. South Sudanese, as it were, are all violent people. This impression is spontaneous because the violence we speak about in South Sudan is the violence that has hit the centre of safety or life protection of the people.

> Violence is an attack on our sense of safety and selfhood. The pain that ensues goes beyond the physical pain of the assault. By being attacked we are reminded of how vulnerable we are. Continuing attacks may cause us to doubt and even abandon the hope which assures our sense of safety and selfhood, since they do not seem to offer the assurance we seek in the midst of these onslaughts.[43]

All those who suffer at the hands of others have a right to expect redress for their sufferings. But unavoidable suffering, borne with patience and without bitterness or desire for revenge, can, of itself, be an ennobling experience of considerable redemptive value. If we do not allow suffering to corrode our humanity it can, instead, enhance our dignity and our feelings of self-worth. From such a position of 'strength in weakness', those sufferers whose hearts and minds have not been twisted by bitterness will be in a much better position, when the opportunity arise, to re-build wholesome and happy lives for themselves, for their families and for their entire communities.

By no means, however, do all of those who suffer great pains and loss at the hands of others possess the mental and spiritual qualities which are needed to avoid the corrosive effects that such suffering can produce on the personality of the victims, and this is especially true where distress, injury, sickness or undernourishment have already seriously weakened the body. Such traumatised individuals and societies need a great deal of support from others before they can hope to be restored to any form of normality. It is generally accepted that the physical sufferings of such people must be attended to but it is not always appreciated that psychological and spiritual treatments and support must swiftly follow.

It has been a common tactic used throughout the history of humankind to plan carefully in order to get rid of a regime that is threatening human existence. This kind of activity is time-consuming and requires a lot of prudence and creativity. We can only overcome suffering from violence

---

[42] From Robert Schreiter's notes. See note 159 above.
[43] Ibid.

by working our way through it. We begin by admitting and acknowledging the violence which has been or that is being done to us, and we obviously must cry out in protest and lamentation against it. Of course, silence is the friend of oppression.[44]

Schreiter encourages us to make efforts to have our complaint raised to the hearing of the world. Maybe it will come to the ear of a God-fearing person or a Good Samaritan, who can speed to our rescue. He emphasises the fact that when the victim cries out, he automatically names the perpetrator of the violence. Crying out gives voice to our pain and calls others to our side, to help us be restored to the larger social network. Crying out is an address, an appeal to God that what we face reaches beyond our ability to cope.[45]

We need God and his presence in our daily life. This stands firm as the ultimate security and peace for humankind. We will see in the following pages God's teaching on the value of reconciliation, a greatly desired gift. This is the right way to handle suffering in order to regain our humanity.

Reconciliation: A Value in Christian Teaching

Reconciliation is at the heart of Christian teaching and mission. The Church walking in the footsteps of her founder and Head, Jesus Christ, is mandated to carry out the same duties as her master. Jesus Christ came into the world for the very purpose of reconciling the broken world with the eternal love of God the Father, and the Church shoulders that mission too. The Fathers at the Second Vatican Council had the same optimism regarding the wellbeing of the creatures of God in all its aspects:

> There must be made available to all people everything necessary for leading a life truly human, such as food, clothing and shelter; the right to choose a state of life freely and to found a family, to respect, to appropriate information, to activity in accord with the upright norm of one's own conscience, to protection of privacy and to rightful freedom in matters religious.[46]

The advent of Jesus Christ the Son of God into the world influenced the world in a typical single mode of reconciliation. Jesus Christ, as truly God became man as we are. He completely reconciled Almighty God with men and women, his creatures. In this way, the love of God for men and women

---

[44] Cf. from Robert Schreiter's notes. See note 159 above
[45] Ibid.
[46] The Vatican II Document referred to is *Gaudium et Spes*, Pastoral Constitution on the Church in the Modern World, n. 26, in: *The Documents of Vatican II*, Paulines Publications Africa, Nairobi 2014.

was clearly revealed. Jesus, in his mission of love for the world, reconciled all the people of different races among themselves and with God. In so doing, he created a unifying platform for all human persons. And finally, Jesus Christ has united all the heavenly and earthly domains and powers through his mission of reconciling the whole world to himself in God.

What is naturally true is that God himself reinforces in our hearts this love for reconciling us with him and others. When possessed by God, the person who has been victimised can make the first move towards reconciliation since he or she has already been molded by God's love and forgiveness. Courage, strength and love enable the wronged person to overlook the past and strive towards wholeness. "For if we were enemies we were reconciled to God through the death of his Son ... we are filled with exultant trust in God, through our Lord Jesus Christ" (Romans 5:10-11).

Following this idea, for us as South Sudanese, and Northern and Western Sudanese, and all the marginalised people of South Sudan who bore and are bearing injustices, only God can touch our hearts to move towards forgiveness and reconciliation. We are not to wait for the aggressors to seek repentance for their atrocities. They will be moved to acknowledge their evildoing only if we, the wronged, can take the initiative and forgive. This is the true procedure of the Christian teaching of reconciliation.

The experience is with the victims of violence. After decades, they surely know how hard it is to take this initiative, and these Christian attitudes are the only motivators of forgiveness that can attract the perpetrators of violence to repent. According to the legal system, the perpetrators of violence should be punished; but the psychologists have not established that punishment is the right method for correcting a person who is in the wrong. And again, experience shows that punishment does not bring people to repentance.[47]

All that the victims of violence need from their spiritual inspiration is to secure the confidence of God's forgiveness in order to move away from sufferings. To do this, the victims must retain their self-image. This, I think, is one of the best medicines to recover from the pain of violence in all its aspects, spiritually and psychologically. The absence of this value can be very detrimental to the victims. The long and complex history of South Sudan may tend to cause many people to breathe threats of vengeance on those whom they consider responsible for their torture and sufferings. Turning away from doing so will be the result of spiritual conversion and commitment.

---

7   From Robert Schreiter's notes. See note 159 above.

It is the order of the day in South Sudan to undervalue the majority of the citizens as hopeless individuals, by treating them as less than human beings and as objects of pity. The South Sudanese Catholic bishops had to warn the Christians about this kind of attitude in their 1984 pastoral letter, "*Lord Come to Our Aid*". This letter was published just a year after the government of President Nimairi implemented the Islamic Sharia law in South Sudan. The bishops wrote:

> If you should be called to suffer for Christ, you must use Christ's way of reacting to suffering, namely acceptance of God's will and patient endurance. Do not, out of cowardice, give way to injustice, violation of human rights, etc. This will only destroy you and others, especially the weak and the ignorant, and will break up the nation…You have to stand for the truth at all times, the truth about yourselves is that you are citizens of this country like anyone else with equal rights to be respected and benefit from what that state makes available, and equal rights to participate fully in the life of the country. There is the truth that you are Africans and Christians, and therefore have the right to live in this country according to your culture, customs and religion. These are your rights; not only as citizens but also as human beings … There is the truth about the other citizens: they have the right to be different. They have the right to live according to their customs, culture and religions, but absolutely no right to impose their customs and religion on you.[48]

Due to the complexity of the long history of violence of South Sudan, some South Sudanese have assumed the position of submissiveness and regard their oppressors as superior to them. They see themselves as being nothing in front of these so-called superiors who keep mistreating them. This is the sad experience of weary and depressed people.

Finally, but not less important, there is the situation where people of one and the same country handle and deal with each other as individuals who are outcast and must be exterminated. Each perceives the other as potentially dangerous. Here there is no relationship but only great fear of the other, all are ignorant of each other. Their mistrust and prejudice increases continuously.

Let us listen to St Paul's words in his Letter to the Ephesians: "For he is peace between us and has made the two into one entity and broken down the barrier which used to keep the two people apart … His purpose in this was, by restoring peace, to create a single New Man out of the two of them … And through the cross to reconcile them both to God in one body" (Ephesians 2:14-15). The reconciliation that Jesus has provided to

---

[48]   Sudan Catholic Bishops Conference, *Letters to the Church of South Sudan*, op. cit., p. 48.

the world is a system of reconciliation that is not only about removing pains, sufferings and violence, or about forcing the oppressors to repent. Reconciliation, more importantly, takes the victims and oppressors into a new world (new creation in Christ) where they both discover new places in their humanity by helping each other.

God leads us out of the state of violence, sufferings and alienation into experiences of reconciliation and peace. The grace received from God makes victims and oppressors open and transformed. But a major success and achievement lies in the fact that both have the opportunity of accepting their humanity.

Reconciliation Must Be Built on Truth

One of the elements that strengthen true reconciliation among people of various backgrounds is telling the truth. This gift can only be asked for, and reinforced by God. As victims of violence, it is hard to take the initiative. Even though we can try to get rid of the impacts of these atrocities, we may not succeed in eradicating these sad episodes completely from ourselves. Parts of them have sunk deep into our subconscious.

In the process of reconciliation, victims and oppressors must target telling the truth: a confession of the truth by both sides to each other. As we have seen in the narration of our South Sudanese history, South Sudanese have sinned and continue to sin against each other in many ways. To tell each other the truth about the wrongs we have done against each other does not necessarily require a technical method of rational problem-solving. We need God's saving grace and light in order to see the truth in the other. This is how we can let God's reconciling grace penetrate into our very own existence and spontaneously into our community life. It is when this experience will dominate our lives that we can begin to carry out a reconciliation process in our society. A reconciled individual or community will have peace and freedom that will never again experience boundaries. Eventually, it will become an on-going experience in that society.[49]

This process of telling each other the truth makes the process of reconciliation an activity of rediscovering, convinced that forgiveness precedes repentance. Then the victims and oppressors will perceive repentance as proof of sincerity in telling the truth to each other in a journey towards

[49] SECAM, Pastoral Letter, "Christ Our Peace" (Eph 2:14)": The Church-as-Family of God, place and sacrament of pardon, Reconciliation and Peace in Africa, SECAM Publications, Kumasi Catholic Press Ltd., October 2001, p. 46.

forgiveness – this is earning forgiveness. Where else can we discover that reconciliation is God's graciousness? Forgiveness is freely given to the needy, it is not earned.[50]

A really Christian attitude of forgiveness has to be interpersonal. What comes to my mind is the heroic act of forgiveness that was manifested by Pope John Paul II. When he narrowly survived an assassin's bullet, right on his hospital bed he inspiringly addressed his atttacker: "My brother, whom I have sincerely forgiven." After some time, Pope John Paul II put his words into action by paying an extraordinary visit to his would-be assassin in prison. The Pope would have had him freed from the prison, had it not been to the obligation of the civil authority. It is possible to forgive.

What do we mean by 'telling each other the truth'? It means that victims must be free to expound the pains suffered and the oppressors must, in free conscience, admit their shortcomings in having inflicted pain on their neighbour. This process of reconciliation in truth means opening one's arms to "the one who is different" with all the ugly experiences of violence, so that one can be born again. In this process, it is quite healthy to allow that, in the words of Schreiter, the victims 'cry and lament', because this is a healing memory.

Finally, truth to oneself and to the rest of humanity constitutes the real reconciliation in which the victims and oppressors become one, a new creation or humanity. Basically, reconciliation ranges high above relieving violence and repentance. Of course, these elements are equally needed in a process of true reconciliation. True reconciliation means crossing over from a world of violence, hatred and wars, into a peaceful and harmonious new world: this is Christian reconciliation. Reconciliation to me is not only restoration, it means to get rid of the old world of vengeance and dwell in a new place.[51]

Churches' Involvement in Reconciliation

Fulfilling their God-given assignments, South Sudanese Churches dedicate their pastoral ministries to the world and search for concrete reconciliation and peace. They have been working hard for peace in South Sudan. They have engaged in direct talks with South Sudanese leaders by writing, approaching or requesting the direct intervention of the international community, persistently asking the neighbouring countries to show solidarity

---

[50]   Cf. Ibid.
[51]   Cf. Ibid.

and cooperation with peace initiatives. For example, in the structure of their Bishops' Conference, the Catholic Bishops have reinforced the Justice and Peace Commission that has sub-offices in all the nine dioceses of South Sudan and Sudan. This commission is very active in grassroots conflict resolution, making reconciliation among different ethnic groups possible.

In their dioceses, and through their pastoral ministries to the war-affected and depressed people, the bishops also engage in dealing with healing and trauma recovery through spiritual and sacramental actions. More particularly, in the major part of the nation, the Churches have engaged in the material development of the people. There is an ecumenical spirit in this regard. All of the churches agree and work in this noble direction of peace (Pentocastal, Evelingelicals, African Inland Churches, Lutherans, Protestants, Catholics, etc). The basic things that people need, such as food, health, schools and social development, have been delivered by the Church throughout the long periods of conflict in South Sudan.

The activities of the Church and the position that the Church holds in the hearts of many suffering South Sudanese are unshakable. The Church is the conscience of many suffering people. For example, for nearly 22 years, to assemble together and celebrate an occasion in larger numbers as non-Muslims in Khartoum and other key cities and towns, was only possible through the Church. Without the Church, it would simply have been an uprising.

What is certain is that South Sudanese bishops have taken sides with the suffering people. And they are approaching the oppressors inviting them to think about the needs of their people and, above all, to aim at true peace. They have developed a strategy of pastoral plans for reconciliation; reconciliation must be done in truth, sincerity and a spirit of solidarity. They have shown a spirit of ecumenical relationship stronger than ever before. An advocacy role has helped to calm much turmoil in South Sudan. One of their ecumenical pastoral letters involving all the leaders of different denominations in South Sudan to the government, the rebel leaders and the international community was entitled '*Enough Is Enough, The War Must Stop*'. In the introductory part, they had this to say:

> We, as Church leaders of South Sudan, are on the ground with the people throughout Sudan and we experience the pain, trauma and yearnings of the grassroots. We speak on behalf of the voiceless and seek to articulate their legitimate concerns. We believe that these concerns and fears have not been adequately addressed and have not been incorporated fully into the peace process. The people of South Sudan demand peace that is just, democratic

and enduring, a peace that will guarantee their security and human rights and allow them to determine their own political future. We are aware of the deep level of mistrust and indeed broken trust within South Sudan.[52]

One thing that is very striking in the bishops' involvement in their reconciliation mission in South Sudan is that the process does not forget the past, it does not cover up or leave any stone unturned in a real fight against injustice, and it constantly calls for justice and truth as prerequisites for reconciliation. In one of their famous letters, *'The Truth Shall Make You Free'* (1991), the bishops explicitly said: "the nation must respect the cultural heritage of each South Sudanese group, without discriminations," etc. Here is their message:

> This is especially true in your right to equal citizenship under the law, your right to the free practice of your religion; your right to defend and preserve your languages and traditional culture and your right as parents to choose the type of education you wish for your children. We Christians appreciate the fact that we live in a multi-cultural and multi-religious society and thus we respect the fact that South Sudanese Muslims want to live according to their belief. We seek to cooperate with them and with all men and women of good will, in all that genuinely contributes to the welfare of all citizens ... We would like to recall here what was said in the pastoral letter of South Sudanese Catholic Bishops "Lord Come to Our Aid" of June 1984, The bishops appealed to you not to be fearful or confused, to trust that truth will triumph and defend your faith against false accusations. Such defense is a God-given right ... In spite of repeated public declarations and assurances by the government that all South Sudanese have equal rights, that there is no discrimination based on religion, race, language or culture, we see clearly that the reality is different. It is very evident that present governmental policies are aimed at creating one nation that is Islamic in religion and Arab in culture, in total disregard of the large number of South Sudanese citizens who are of other faiths and cultures.[53]

In their 1994 pastoral letter, *'Lend Me Your Ears'*, the bishops were asking for human understanding and solidarity in finding an equal ground for the search for peace in South Sudan:

> Real and fruitful dialogue is however possible only if: The parties concerned usually listen to one another. The purpose of listening is for the parties to come to know and understand one another. They listen not only to the word spoken but to the person speaking. For persons involved in dialogue bring with them their background, their problems, their experiences, their feelings, and their

---

[52] THE CATHOLIC AND EPISCOPAL BISHOPS OF SOUTH SUDAN, Joint Pastoral Letter: *Enough Is Enough The War Must Stop,* Uganda, August 1st 2003.

[53] SUDAN CATHOLIC BISHOPS CONFERENCE, *Letters to the Church of South Sudan,* op. cit., p. 160.

history. True listening demands that the parties put themselves into each other's shoes and try to understand not only what is said, but also why it is said, and why it is said that way ... True dialogue can therefore take place only if all the parties are sincerely and honestly eager to learn together, and to search earnestly for truth and unity. Dialogue will fail if any one of the parties claims to know the whole truth and so begins to dictate to the others. In dialogue all the participants are partners. They meet on *LEVEL GROUND*, not from above.[54]

"For that the Church is the conscience of the society. She may discover that the wall dividing the one nation passes exactly through the middle of the Church."[55] In the first place, it should come as no surprise for one to discover that some well-known individuals of the Church can be drawn to work alongside the very government that is responsible for the sufferings of its people, just to win some benefits or for prudence sake. Secondly, some Church leaders or personnel may choose to side with the opposite of what the ruling government and warring groups are standing for, for the sake of advocacy, to raise their voice on behalf of the voiceless. But they do it at the expense of their life, risking imprisonment, exile, torture, intimidation, abuse, etc. A third category is that of some Church leaders who choose to collaborate with the oppressive government or with any form of leadership of that nature, in order to secure peace. These cause a split to occur in the Church, because some members – priests and outspoken priests, sisters (nuns) or lay Christians – may become opponents to such a move, which, as a matter of fact, has the hearts of the majority. Reconciliation is not simple. It must be gradual and careful. I consider it quite necessary and equally important for the Church to be reconciled from within, in order to be a true agent or minister of reconciliation.[56]

Finally, in their teaching, South Sudanese bishops have kept to the truth of the Gospel and have helped all South Sudanese people realise their need for forgiveness, because we are all sinners. The Church, right from the day of Pentecost, has maintained her position of preaching the Good News of Jesus' resurrection. "Men of Israel, listen to what I am going to say: Jesus the Nazarene was a man commended to you by God by the miracles ... This man who was put into your power by the deliberate intention ... But God raised him to life" (Acts of the Apostles 2:22-24).

[54] Ibid., pp, 109-110.
[55] From Robert Schreiter's notes. See note 159 above.
[56] Ibid.

Reconciliation after the War

What comes to the mind when one hears of post-war reconstruction? What are the immediate challenges of the aftermath of a devastating civil war? Most often, there is much focus on material reconstruction. These entail lobbying for political positions, seeking relief for rehabilitation, struggling for position, particularly by those who believe they have been more engaged for peace or in the revolution, sidelining those who seem to have contributed less and above all scaling the returnees or refugees, mild diplomatic revenge on some ethnic groups or community who are held responsible for some loss, etc. These situations and others are likely to provoke violence again.[57]

One of the main preoccupations of postwar restoration, the soul of reconstruction, in other words, reconciliation, which is more spiritual. If this spirit is lacking, there is no rebuilding. Thoughts, attitudes, relationships, cultural and religious heritages, social progress, institutions, are elements that compose the soul and spirit of a given society. These must be very active in the restoration of a nation after a conflict or war. In the same way, a good government is of great help after war is over and it is time for peace and rebuilding. I think it would be a lack of wisdom and a tremendous error if the current peace negotiators and the international community would wish to impose their system of democracy, their way of doing things, and of practicing reconciliation in South Sudan in the name of universal principles. South Sudan should be free to choose what is appropriate according to the dynamics of its own spirit of reconciliation and development in coordination.

The reality of the conflicts which have been endured by ordinary South Sudanese must be reviewed in the process of reconstruction. What is necessary is to revive a correct concept of the meaning of life that has been lost for centuries by South Sudanese, making it possible for them to regain the dignity of the human person and a sense of community and nation. This will need a well-based and organised social and political structure. It would be scarcely possible, indeed miraculous, for such an achievement to become realised outright. Abomination and catastrophic civil strife, violence of all kinds throughout the history of South Sudan, cannot be terminated or rubbed out through peace negotiations, not even after having animated the oppressors and evil perpetrators for some years. It is unthinkable to believe that a well-founded resolution can automatically

---

[57]   ST AUGUSTINE, *The City of God*, Book XV, Chap 4.

fill the gap of disintegration and violence caused by what has happened during an entire period of history. It needs time for evil-doers to realise the need for peace and reconciliation.

It is incredibly important to continue the push for reconciliation, and make the majority of people realise where they are, what they are actually missing, what has been happening to them throughout history, what they have lost, and why they have become the objects of sympathy. It is natural that humans are capable enough of feeling that they have ceased to be human. This feeling is the presupposition of a genuine reconciliation and reconstruction. For in this feeling humanity makes itself heard in its longing for a meaning of life, for community and personality. It has always belonged and still belongs to the great hopes of mankind, that, as new generations grow up, they may be able to receive new creative stamina.

Furthermore, another outstanding hope is that the religious and cultural traditions that are still alive in our society can continue to inspire and animate our nation. The Christian message can be very effective during the reconstruction period, especially when it is inserted into the very centre of life of the current society. This is what Jesus meant when he said: "If your brother does something wrong, rebuke him, and if he is sorry, forgive him. And if he wrongs you seven times a day and seven times comes back to you and says, 'I am sorry' you must forgive him" (Luke 17:4). The Christians must be co-workers in the Church and bring this message to all. It would be very effective, especially if backed by the Churches that enjoy ecumenical unity. But Churches are not the whole of our culture, they are only a small portion of our huge secular society. It is to be remembered that little or nothing can be achieved without the collaboration of the secular powers in a work of reconciliation and restoration.

As John Paul II affirms:

> The aspiration for peace that you share with all men and women corresponds to an initial call by God to form a single family of brothers and sisters, created in the image of the same Father ... the difficulties we encounter in our journey towards peace are linked partly to our weakness as creatures, who must necessarily advance by slow progressive steps.[58]

The Azande famous parable puts it well: "*Sungo sungo na bi rumburu ru aru*" (literally it means that the one who sits down firmly clearly sees the bystander). It means that learning to wait involves being calm and comfortable with ourselves. It also involves waiting and listening to God's

---

[58] Ibidem.

wisdom to guide us to behave wisely. This attitude is very necessary for the reconciliation and restoration of a nation after violence. It allows for painful memories to heal and give way to allow reconciliation and peace to well up in each heart. This, precisely, is Christian reconciliation; this is its message.

Justice is interwoven with power, since power by its application implies justice. Vice versa, justice by its definition implies power, and both of them are implied in charity, which is love, the ultimate longing of human beings to live in a reconciled and peaceful society.

In short, the post-war economic situation of South Sudan's people, the real victims of the long sufferings of violence in South Sudan, is the real key to the future. We know this from our past experience, where we saw that without an economic, social and spiritual disintegration, before, during and after independence, no form of violence would have arisen.

All the following: economic, social justice and religions, spiritual animation for a true spirit of reconciliation and peace can turn the post-war nation into a peaceful and progressive one. It needs a new marriage of power or authority and justice, in the spiritual unity of charity, to act as a *springboard* for reconciliation. Jesus gives his golden rule as a measuring rod to humanity, to treat each other with respect and love. "So always treat others as you would like them to treat you; that is the law and the prophets" (Matthew 7:12). All the believers of God, who may be worshipping him in various ways and means, have this rule for their community, so it applies for all.

The Potential of Religions in Reinforcing Reconciliation

South Sudanese people are naturally in the supernatural Being, in other words in God Almighty. Traditional religion, the Islamic religion and the Christian religion all adore God in their own way. These religions have a strong influence on the individual lives of each South Sudanese and have become a very strong cultural heritage for our people. Religion has a great influence on politics and is considered to be the third main reason (after economic and social justice) for the ongoing escalating violence in South Sudan.

Despite the rich spiritual nourishment that religion can offer, some of these religions have developed radicalism, fanaticism and sectarianism that continue to widen the gap in relationships, brotherhood and nationalism more and more each day. The consequence of this has been wars, killings, vengeance and violence of all sorts. Because of this, too, Sudan is experiencing a lot of international isolation, and an absence of peace and of human development.

More importantly, these religions are very rich and carry the ultimate and profound destiny, dignity and meaning of the human person in the world. They help men and women rediscover themselves in union with their common origin who is God, the Creator of them all. South Sudanese cannot deny the privileges and prosperity they have achieved through these religions. I think South Sudanese already possess the raw materials that are opportunities from which all can benefit. The message of love, justice and peace that each of these religions preaches and teaches, can be used to heal and reconcile the destroyed nation. During his visit to South Sudan, on February 10th 1993, His Holiness Pope John Paul II, in view of the religious conflictive situation, told the religious leaders in South Sudan:

> I have looked forward to this meeting with you, the leaders of various religions professed by the people of South Sudan. My pastoral visit to the Catholic Church in this nation gives me the opportunity to extend the hand of friendship to you, and to express the hope that all the citizens of South Sudan, irrespective of differences between them, will live in harmony and in mutual cooperation for the common good ... Religion permeates all aspects of life in society, and citizens need to accept one another, with all their differences of language, customs, culture and belief, if civic harmony is to be maintained. Religious leaders play an important role in fostering that harmony.[59]

I am not prepared to go into a detailed teaching of the doctrines of these religions, but I am interested in what they teach about justice and peace through reconciliation. I know, as many others can confirm, that these religions are capable enough of contributing to genuine peace building. If, based on their religions, they will believe in the value of justice and peace, the right value of the human person and the necessity of reconciliation for all, then there will be a way forward.

South Sudanese traditional religion is the earliest religion. South Sudanese people in their various ethnic groups believe in a supernatural being who is held in high esteem, who is a reason for their being and has created the world for their enjoyment and for their lives. He is a God who provides all good things, a God who blesses and a God who is capable of punishing evil and individual sin, community and world sins. People who follow this faith quite concretely build their community, individual and

---

[59]   JOHN PAUL II, in SUDAN CATHOLIC BISHOPS' CONFERENCE, *Letters to the Church of South Sudan*, op. cit., n. 175.

family life on the principles of this faith. These people have the drive to live in peace and harmony. They have a strong sense of justice and peace through reconciliation, reinforced and guided by the elders of their communities. In the past, the kings, chiefs or elders of the communities were called upon by the obligation of the taboo to offer maximum protection to their subjects. Violence or catastrophy of any kind was often believed to be a punishment of the community by the ancestors. In this case the community, led by the elders, was obliged to offer sacrifices of repentance and forgiveness. Such prayers for the individual and the community's sins normally made peace and progress reign among the people.

Some of the powerful elements that can reinforce peace building, justice and reconciliation and that are active in the traditional society are community life, the extended family, and the influence of the elders of the community. At the grassroots level, these elements can be very easily realised and reinforced. Alliance and peace pacts with other communities in conflict are always the pride of a given society under the patronage of leaders.

This religion advocates pardon, forgiveness and, above all, a spirit of reconciliation, which makes it hard to revert to violence with the old opponents. Without this search for permanent peace and reconciliation, it will be very hard to realise true peace. As a minority in South Sudan, traditionalist believers have been terribly ignored. Their presence needs to be enhanced in order to be active in their traditional role as constructors of peace at the grassroots level.

Christianity is the second religion in the chronological order and the first foreign religion in South Sudan. This faith has been abundantly embraced by South Sudanese people and is the second major religion, followed by 25% of the population. This revealed religion occupies a dominant place in world history. God willed his created world and humanity to remain reconciled to him. Even though men had sinned against his endless love, he sent his beloved Son Jesus Christ, in the likeness of man, to save and reconcile the wounded humanity to its origin – God. To accomplish this, Jesus chose the human condition of pain by dying on the cross for the salvation of all. He reconciled men with their neighbours and with himself in God the Father.

Jesus Christ entrusted his Church with the duty to carry out this redemptive work of reconciliation and salvation: "Go therefore, and make disciples of all the nations, and baptise them in the name of the Father and of the Son and of the Holy Spirit" (Mt 28:18-20). In her prophetic mission, the Church in many occasions identified herself with the victims of humanity and condemned all forces that tended to dehumanise people

The Church tries to announce the message of justice and peace through reconciliation wherever violence and inhuman conditions are curtailing the basic values of human rights. The Church, in many circumstances, advocates respect, love, solidarity and oneness for humankind. Likewise, the Churches, through their leaders, have devoted their pastoral ministry to the message of love, justice and reconciliation for peace throughout the lasting period of violence. It is to be remembered also that the 1972 Peace Accord that lasted for ten years was the initiative of the World Council of Churches, the Verona Fathers, etc. The established role of the Catholic bishops in looking for the possibility of peace is the proof that the Church has quite some influence in trying to resolve the ongoing crisis.

The achievement of Christian reconciliation is something that cannot be imposed, as we saw in the previous pages. Rather, it is a reality that flourishes from within the self, promoted by God, as a result of a spiritual deepening. This energises the victim of violence to go and utter forgiveness to his assumed oppressor. This unique Christian attitude can inspire the oppressor to repent. This act should not be confused with cowardice; it is a believer's true attitude.

If all Christians would allow themselves to be touched and molded by God, who ignites love, forgiveness and reconciliation, forgiveness can easily come about. But what is involved here, is the way this behaviour will be perceived by whoever belongs to a different faith and believes you are his enemy. Can Muslims perceive these attitudes in the South Sudanese case? I think it is an important point of concern that is needed for there to be a spirit of dialogue among the followers of these religions.

The Muslim faith was the last of these three religions to enter South Sudan. Islam is a religion that has a very strong doctrine and tradition, like Christianity. It holds a strong faith in the one God who is identified as a merciful God. A contemporary Muslim writer sums up the meaning of Islam thus:

> Islam stands for "a commitment to surrender one's will to the Will of God and as such be at peace with the Creator and with all that has been created by him. It is through submission to the Will of God that peace is produced. Harmonisation of our will with the Will of God brings about harmonisation of different spheres of life under an all-embracing ideal."[60]

---

[60] Ch. Troll, "Islam and Reconciliation", in *Encounter* (Documents for Muslim-Christian Understanding), Pontificio Istituto di Studi arabi e d'islamistica, Rome1984, p. 4.

Islam has taught its followers the notion of justice, peace and reconciliation. It is clear that these elements are directed to Muslims among themselves. Justice, peace and reconciliation towards, or with, non-Muslims are only being tolerated. Cooperation and relationships with non-Muslims can be accommodated.

Some followers of Islam have become fundamentalists; this gives an impression of violence, over and above the fact that Islam cannot separate politics from religious activities. However, daily contacts with devout Muslims show that they are quite open. There are many possibilities for a life in coexistence. Many Muslims are moderate and this can reinforce dialogue and inter-religious activities for the sake of peace. Sayyed Quth, who made a special study on the theory of war in Islam, pinpoints the conditions needed before a Muslim should go into war:

In Islam, peace is the rule, and war is a necessity that should not be resorted to, but to achieve the following objectives: to uphold the rule of Allah on earth, so that the complete submission of men would be exclusively to him; to eliminate oppression, extortion and injustice by instituting the word of Allah; to achieve the human ideas that are considered by Allah as the aims of life, and to secure people against terror, coercion and injury.[61]

But the point is that in all these religions the message of love, justice and peace, respect for human dignity can be found. Therefore the followers can make use of these rich traditions and religious inspiration to heal themselves of all the evils of violence that have befallen their nation. The Catholic bishops of South Sudan in their pastoral letter of June 1993 entitled *'Blessed Are the Peace-Makers'*, called for reconciliation and peace, encouraging everybody to take an active part in searching for peace:

Our appeal is that since each one of us is liable to engage in activities or develop a mentality that does not favour the cause of peace but rather the cause of war, we appeal here to all South Sudanese of good will. Although responsibility for peace varies according to each one's position in society, and each one's capabilities, there is no one who can withdraw himself from bearing responsibility for peace without causing problems in society ... we appeal to both Muslims and Christians to live their convictions seriously and faithfully. For both Islam and Christianity profess to be religions of justice, reconciliation, love, peace and brotherhood. Both profess faith in God who is all powerful, merciful, compassionate and just. How can we be believers, if we practice and promote so much cruelty, injustice and falsehood?[62]

---

[61] SAYYED QUTH, *Islam and Universal Peace,* The American Trust Publication, Indiana 1977, p. 9.
[62] SUDAN CATHOLIC BISHOPS' CONFERENCE, *Letters to the Church of South Sudan,* op. cit., p. 150, § 4.

Gestures of inter-religious dialogue, joint commissions for the cause of peace in the country, and tolerance among the followers towards others are activities that promote peace. Peace is possible if the religious leaders of the Traditional, Muslim and Christian religions, together with their disciples, join hands to rid South Sudan of violence. They have a tremendous influence on the politics and government of this nation. Through them peace is possible.

Peace Is Possible

Jesus, for the love of saving the fallen world, had to pass through all kinds of pain, passion, violence and death on the cross. On his journey towards his violent death, Jesus never used violence to defend himself, nor did he plead with his close friends to defend him forcefully. This violent death in all its ugliness was undergone out of love. Jesus asked Peter, one of his Apostles who had wanted to defend him, to put his sword back into its case: "Suddenly, one of the followers of Jesus grasped his sword and drew it; he struck the high priest's servant and cut off his ear. Jesus then said, 'put your sword back, for all who draw the sword will die by the sword" (*Matthew* 26:51-53). To completely overcome the power of violence, Jesus rose from death. His resurrection has become the joy of humanity; everyone has life in him in all its fullness. All is made possible; an everlasting peace awaits all men of good will. All the believers are invited to participate in his saving mission of salvation, of peace, justice and reconciliation.

The Church has the obligation to carry out this message of love, truth, justice and peace, which a profoundly troubled world is so much in need of, and this is even truer for South Sudan, which has been deprived of these privileges for decades. The victory of Jesus over death and violence is consoling and good news for us in South Sudan: one day, some time, we will overcome these tragedies.

The ongoing crisis of violence that we are witnessing in South Sudan is a reminder that to build peace is a never-ending job and that the greatest challenge remains that of challenging violence in all its forms. The continued contradictions of South Sudan, the increasing differences in the distribution of wealth, of power and provision of social services, lack of equal opportunity for all and respect for the dignity of the human person, make frustration grow and keep creating increasing risks. The supreme reign of profits of all kinds and the breakdown of the social fabric lead to the dominance of strength over justice. What then will enable us to keep going? Christians know the secret: the source of peace is reconciliation. Daniel Berrigan summarises it thus:

> A different social compact, implying a far different humanism, has been proposed by Jesus. "Serve one another" In effect: This is the way that best responds both to your nature and to the will of God. Moreover, and of equal import, this is the way that most sharply sets you off from the brutalities of secular power.[63]

Peace is possible because the risen Lord has won eternal life for all and the made it possible to live as one reconciled family of God. As such, all have the capacity to see others with the eyes of Christ, which allows us to meet them not with mistrust, but with a spirit of welcoming and of listening. Others are no longer strangers, enemies, oppressors, competitors, or a burden, but a gift. This noble attitude is expressed by Albert Nolan, who emphasised that:

> Real solidarity begins when we recognise together the advantages and disadvantages of our different social backgrounds and present realities and the quite different roles that we shall therefore have to play while we commit ourselves together to the struggle against oppression.[64]

In our situation of various backgrounds, with religious and cultural diferences, diversity becomes the field where a communion is worked out; not the virtual unity of the information highway, nor that of a uniform, globalised subculture reduced to its lowest common denominator, but a communion rooted in the unique central core of a faith that comes to quicken and give meaning to our most intimate hope, allowing us to open up and grow by taking up and welcoming the living gifts specific to the traditions of others.

Aware of the enormous riches that can descend on a community of believers, people who trace their all to God the Creator and Maker of all, one can convincingly say that *peace is possible.* We have a genuine reason to hope for peace and tranquility in South Sudan. Going meditatively through the pages of this book, we can all say it is right and genuine to hope. After all, nobody can live without hope, even if it were only for the smallest things that give some satisfaction, even in the worst of conditions, even in poverty, sickness and social failure. Without hope, the tension of

---

[63] DANIEL BERRIGAN, *Whereon to Stand: The Acts of the Apostles and Ourselves,* Fortkamp Publishing Baltimore 1991, p. 20.

[64] Albert Nolan, o.p., who was elected Master General of the Dominican Order and resigned after one day to continue his work with the poor in South Africa, is quoted in CHED MYERS, Who will roll away the stone?, op. cit., p. 282.

our life towards the future would vanish, and with it, so would life itself. We would end in despair, a word that originally meant "without hope" or deadly indifference. Therefore I want to ask the question: Do we have a right to hope? Is there justified hope for each of us, for nations such as ours, which have seen nothing but misery and killing? Do we have a right to hope, even against hope? Even against the reality of death?

If we work hard, surely our hope will reach its target. As John Paul II affirms in his 2005 Message for World Peace, where he rekindles hope in a desperate humanity:

> Based on the certainty that evil will not prevail, Christians nourish an invincible hope which sustains their efforts to promote justice and peace. Despite the personal and social sins which mark all human activity, hope constantly gives new impulse to the commitment to justice and peace, as well as firm confidence in the possibility of building a better world.[65]

Agents of peacebuilding must be committed. We have noticed the hard pastoral work that has been carried out by South Sudanese Catholic Bishops in their efforts to bring peace to South Sudan. This explains the role of the Church throughout the world to stand beside the weary and the suffering, to bring the Good News of peace, which her founder Jesus Christ accomplished through his passion, death on the cross and resurrection, for the salvation of all humankind.

SECAM said:

> The Church-as-family of God is the place and the instrument of this peace of Christ, it is the "sacrament – a sign and instrument, that is – of communion with God and of the unity among all men" (LG 1). It continues the work of its Divine Founder, who died to gather into one the scattered children of God (Jn 11:52).[66]

Reinforcement of justice, authority and peace will have to rest with the South Sudanese people if the peace is to be meaningful and lasting. The potential is there, within the circle of the South Sudanese community, in both their religious leaders and community elders. If the process of reconciliation is taken seriously, if we will make a generous use of our spiritual riches, it is very easy to say: Peace is possible. We have genuine reasons to truly hope.

[65] John Paul II, *Message for World Peace Day 2005*, n. 11.
[66] SECAM, Pastoral Letter, "Christ Our Peace" (Eph 2:14)": The Church-as-Family of God, place and sacrament of pardon, Reconciliation and Peace in Africa, SECAM Publications, Kumasi Catholic Press Ltd., October 2001, p. 43.

Questions for Reflection

1. Why is it appropriate to think and speak about justice and peace through reconciliation at this time?

2. Can you see the notion of justice, peace and reconciliation as the ultimate cause for ending the long South Sudanese violence in your immediate circle of experience?

3. Our studies have shown that the absence of justice begets evil, but then how can justice be reinforced and who can sustain it in a nation?

4. One of the impacts of the long history of violence is trauma. Techniques can applied to rid the people of the effects of trauma. In this regard, who can guarantee the implementation of reconciliation and peace?

5. Peacebuilding must be a given job, to help reduce the burning desires for revenge, for war, and instead inspire people to contruct a culture of peace. But, if authority is the only power that can have immediate influence, who can empower those in authority, and how can they be influenced to acquire the quality of peacebuilding?

6. Do you have some practical examples and proposals through which our religious heritage of South Sudanese Traditional Religion, Christian and Muslims religions, can promote South Sudan's search for genuine and lasting peace?

7. What can South Sudan do to prevent another war?

8. This book proposes that a journey through justice, peace and reconciliation, according to Christ' example, is in our best interest. In whose interest? Do you think the message is valid for all humanity – for all to love and forgive?

Conclusion

I wish to conclude this book with some brief reflections on the five important stages of the fifth chapter of this book:

- The prehistory and events leading up to South Sudan's independence;
- The aftermath of independence;
- The impact of the conflict and South Sudan at the crossroad of violence,
- Reconciliation, the responsibility of all; and
- Reconciliation, healing, gift of God to all humankind.

Events Leading Up to Independence

My genuine trust and interest is in acknowledging that the past as a transition to a peaceful future has reinforced the project of this book. In paying attention to or re-reading South Sudanese history, it becomes obvious to me that the past paves the way to the future, our history is a necessity for a prosperous future to occur. A situation such as the one that has been devastating South Sudan requires an enormous move ahead, however modest it may sound to outsiders. It will take a long time before there is forgiveness, a longer time still for reconciliation to happen and then further time for gradual and absolute healing.

The hasty preparation and coming of South Sudanese independence left many substantial issues unaddressed. Issues such as the identity of South Sudanese, untapped historical deposits of painful memories, shared visions, commitment to the rule of law, institutional structural construction, peace-building requirements, etc, and other omissions, cost South Sudan its peace within only 29 months of achieving independence.

The Aftermath of Independence

This period is characterised as the period of great negligence. Since July 9th 2011, when South Sudan attained its independence, political stability and total peace for its citizens were never fully realised.

Hence, we need a second reading of our history, so that we can compose a new chapter of political stability, security, freedom, social transformation and peace. If we want to look for the real causes behind this devastating failure to bring about justice and peace through reconciliation, we have to adjust the existing differences, such as religious and political ideologies, wealth sharing and equality in power delegation. Inclusivitity and full participation must be part and parcel of nation building, where the diversity of the people of this nation is realised and celebrated. This will require our solidarity, which we have to inject into the system to accommodate every South Sudanese in the new national character and national rebuilding.

In a complex situation, such as ours, a possibility of agreement must be found in a genuine compromise: the need to compromise is regrettable, but it is a moral, noble as well as a political need. I think it is hard to be virtuous in this global world by doing justice mathematically. One recommendation seems correct: to abandon it to the virtue of political prudence to acknowledge this.

The Impact of Violence

Civil war has inflicted enormous poverty in South Sudan. The humanitarian fate has been aggravated beyond imagination. War has brought the people to starvation; it has meant enormous destitution for millions of people, especially society's most delicate ones: women and children.

The ongoing conflict has manifold dimensions. Moreover, it is not limited to a specific zone or to a certain population. It bisects across groups, regions, ethnic, and social strata, causing a difficult and complex situation, but one should not call it "impossible". There is a demanding need for political stability.

One of the instruments that can reverse the course of violence is to struggle and win political stability. The way forward can and must be the following:

• Negotiating the substantial issues at the core of the conflict between the people of South Sudan, then securing a workable solution;
• Obtaining immediate humanitarian assistance for the weaker ones in society, such as the elderly, women and children;
• Finding a common denominator for the role of religion in South Sudanese society, basically it would need a lot of inter-religious sharing and dialogue;

- The economy must be given firm and improved performance; and
- There must be proper formation of the national character of South Sudanese people. This must include, among other things, peace education, trauma counselling programmes, academic excellence for the children and the young.

Reconciliation is obviously required in the South Sudanese situation, where suffering has moral connotations, largely defining circumstances that leave suffering uncomforted. The possibility of acknowledging the importance of reconciliation and forgiveness for the sake of life and survival as the only alternative to violence is surely the best recommendation for all people of good will.

Reconciliation Is a Responsibility

This study has made me realise that it is a responsibility to forgive and to repent. When one acknowledges and assumes his responsibility in all its aspects, one becomes answerable.

The responsibility required in seeking reconciliation lies equally for both the perpetrators of violence and its victims. The issue that has to be understood well is that the distinction that has to be made in any conflict between guilt and responsibility, both while the violence is still active, as well as when it has ended. I, or my family, can naturally feel guilty about the situation: things that have been inflicted on me, or maybe on my name, even if I did not do anything wrong myself, even before I was born, or perhaps I am a guilty survivor or beneficiary of the agony of other people. For this matter, I am surely not responsible for what my parents did; but I should become responsible if I take revenge for the evil they have suffered.

In their need for a lasting peace, South Sudanese must look at the basic socio-political and geographical make up of their country. This will surely reveal the reasons for our failure to sustain our country's security and stability. We need to start afresh, to promote first and foremost peace, respect for human rights and human dignity, respect for a cultural and religious plurality and a desire for justice and equality.

Another profound search for peace in South Sudan has to lie with the people. While a political agreement has to rest in the hands of politicians and political leaders, the alternative way forward lies in the active participation of the people at the grassroots level. This method has to be applied to all South Sudanese, to help melt down that national mistrust and prejudice that is the product of history. The pursuit of peace is the responsibility of all South Sudanese.

This move must, first of all, be based on effectively building a mutual trust and respect between the people of South Sudan, though they come from different backgrounds.

Reconciliation, a Gift of God to Humanity

It goes without saying that all South Sudanese citizens have been affected by the cumulative effects of decades of violence. Countless people who have lived through the troubled years in South Sudan hold, with conviction, that they have been innocently harmed, and as such many sustain or harbour a festering anger against the leadership, politicians, institutions, groups or individuals. Many people do not seem to foresee an end to violence, and sadly enough, do not trust the political organisations. Other people entertain a feeling of the harm that has been done to others who were bereaved, injured, or suffered human rights violations. This kind of harm, committed against one member of the community by others, takes on a wider significance in violently divided societies such as South Sudan. It is perceived as harm to every member of that community. Anger, fear, and grievance become public and communal, while perhaps only long-term grief and most forms of remorse are relegated to the private domain.

Our history of political violence is not limited to the persons killed or injured. The whole of South Sudan, with all its social and political organisations, have been modeled or manipulated by the acute divisions within society and have adjusted themselves in response to the ongoing violent conflict.

Since South Sudanese are religiously engaged, there are many healthy reasons for South Sudanese traditionalists, the Muslims and the Christian communities to engage in a pro-active duty to join hands and work together. These religions are incredibly rich in their teaching as far as human duties to God and one's neighbour are concerned. These spiritual resources must be utilised for the reconstruction of a South Sudan characterised by permanent peace and prosperity, where every person will live and grow together in a spirit of love, forgiveness, equality and freedom, brotherhood and mutual respect. SECAM confirms the techniques of reconciliation:

Peace of Christ means dialogue, communication, reconciliation between God and men and between men themselves. It means harmony and understanding, solidarity, acceptance and interaction, cooperation and sharing.[67]

The responsibility of securing peace after this long conflict rests heavily on the shoulders of the Church. In order to gain back their humanity, South Sudanese should rely on the pastoral counselling of the Church. The trauma healing, counselling to heal the memories, and the celebration of the sacraments are essential requisites to recover from the aftermath of war and violence. These programmes must include all who have survived this violence, adults and children, government officials, military personnel, civilian population, etc.

Finally, the current tragic crisis in South Sudan is measuring out a test for our national conscience, our Christian conscience, Muslim and traditionalists' consciences, our feeling of responsibility, our love. The outcome of the crisis or violence does not depend only on statesmen and politicians. It depends on the Churches and Christians, on Muslims and Mosques, as well as on other believers too. But, most of all, it will depend on him, who is present to everyone, everywhere and who permits everything, as the Treasurer of goods and Giver of life, if we open our hearts to him. That is why we will keep hoping, even when there is little hope, and rejoice in him when we are sadly downcast. One of the four Evangelists of the Holy Bible, St Matthew, concluded his gospel with Jesus' last message for mission and action to his apostles: "Go, therefore, and make disciples of all nations" (Matthew 28:19). Jim Douglass interprets this as follows:

Transform the nations of the world by teaching them to turn from the logic of violence to the logic of love and forgiveness. That is the nature of the new age begun in Jesus' resurrection of all peoples and nations in a forgiving, reconciled humanity.[68]

---

[67] SECAM, Pastoral Letter, "Christ Our Peace" (Eph 2:14)": The Church-as-Family of God, place and sacrament of pardon, Reconciliation and Peace in Africa, SECAM Publications, Kumasi Catholic Press Ltd,, October 2001, p. 43.
[68] JIM DOUGLASS, *The Non-Violent Coming of God,* Orbis Books, Maryknoll, New York 1991, p. 178.

Prayer by Fr Robert Schreiter

LORD,

penetrate these murky corners where we hide our memories and tendencies on which we do not care to look, but which we will not yield freely up to you, that you may purify them and transmute them:

- *the persistent grudge,*
- *the half-acknowledged enmity which is still smouldering,*
- *the bitterness of that loss we have not turned into sacrifice,*
- *the private comfort we cling to,*
- *the secret fear of failure which saps our initiative and is really inverted pride,*
- *the pessimism which is an insult to your joy.*

LORD,

we bring all these to you, and we review them with shame and penitence in your steadfast light.

Index of Names,
Places and Major Themes

United Nations 22
Unity 17, 27, 28, 35, 38, 46, 49, 50, 99, 101, 102, 108, 109

V

Vengeance 93, 96, 102
Victim 44, 45, 50, 77, 78, 84, 85, 86, 87, 88, 89, 92, 105

W

Wau 19

Y

Yambio 8, 19
Yei 19